perfect palettes
for painting rooms

ROCKPORT

perfect palettes

for painting rooms

PLUS COMPLETE DECORATING GUIDELINES

Bonnie Rosser Krims

GLOUCESTER MASSACHUSETTS

ROCKPORT PUBLISHERS

First published in the United States of America by
Rockport Publishers, Inc.
33 Commercial Street
Gloucester, Massachusetts 01930-5089
Telephone: (978) 282-9590
Fax: (978) 283-2742
www.rockpub.com

Library of Congress Cataloging-in-Publication Data
Krims, Bonnie Rosser.
   Perfect palettes for painting rooms: plus complete decorating guidelines / Bonnie Rosser Krims.
       p.   cm.
   ISBN 1-56496-996-7 (pbk.)
   1. Color in interior decoration. 2. House painting. I. Title.
NK2115.5.C6K75 2003
747'.94—dc21   2003002175
                                                               CIP

ISBN 1-56496-996-7

10 9 8 7 6 5 4 3 2 1

Design: Peter King & Company
Cover Image: Bobbie Bush Photography, www.bobbiebush.com

Grateful acknowledgment is given to the following for permission to use their paint color numbers, though the four-color process colors used in printing this book may not exactly match each manufacturer's paint chip colors: Benjamin Moore and Company; California Paints, California Paints' Historic Colors of America (California Products Corporation); Glidden Paint; Pratt and Lambert Paints (The Sherwin-Williams Company); PPG Architectural Finishes, Inc. (PPG Industries, Inc./Pittsburgh Paints).

Paint manufacturers routinely reevaluate their color systems. Consequently, you may encounter a few colors for which sample paint chips are unavailable. However, paint in these colors will still be available; simply use the discontinued color numbers to obtain the paint from your paint store.

Printed in Singapore

contents

introduction

Have you ever visited someone's home and said, "Wow, I just love the way this place looks," knowing that its occupants decorated it themselves? You were left wishing, "If only my home could look this good. But how in the world could I do this?" Maybe you can't hire a full-service designer or a professional paint color consultant. Still, you want your home to look pulled together and inviting, reflecting your personal touches throughout.

We know that paint color alone can profoundly enhance our rooms, and we may have a strong desire to use more interesting paint colors in our home. We want a sense of continuity of color and design from room to room. Still, we can't figure out how to go about doing it.

While we may be clear on what we love and have ideas about how we want our home to look, most of us are faced with these decorating decisions. We already have many possessions that are unrelated in style and color. We may like a variety of furniture styles and home accessory items of different origins but can't figure out how to combine them in an attractive way; instead, they seem to detract from the continuity of our decor. We accumulate these things over the years, and our homes get bogged down by the clutter. Short of tossing everything out and starting from scratch, we can't imagine what to do.

All decorating is
about memories.

—SISTER PARISH

Perfect Palettes for Painting Rooms has
the answers. It will empower you to
create a wonderful environment. Your
home will be versatile. It will be a great
place for entertaining friends as well
as nurturing a sense of serenity and
family soul.

My first book, *The Perfect Palette*
(Warner Books, 1998), focused on paint
color schemes and provided general
decorating and accessorizing guidelines.
Many readers commented that they loved
the paint colors but wanted more decorating and accessorizing advice. *Perfect
Palettes for Painting Rooms* was written
to reflect the updated interior paint
color palettes of your favorite paint
manufacturers and to meet your need
for practical, detailed decorating and
accessorizing guidelines. For those of
you choosing paint colors for the exterior
of your house, please refer to my second
book, *The Perfectly Painted House*
(Rockport Publishers, 2001).

Every room in your home can be upgraded
within your budget if you follow the
guidelines in this book, apply some
personal ingenuity, and trust the
creativity you discover in yourself during
the process. All the paint colors
suggested have been used successfully in
the homes of my clients. I carefully
chose each color scheme to ensure a
pleasing, cohesive look. In addition, I
provide comprehensive, practical information on furnishings and accessories
and how to choose them. You can create
a self-expressive environment using the
home furnishings you already own or
take an economical approach when
purchasing furniture or accessories by
investing in a few high-quality basics
and filling in with budget items of sound
structure and good design. The result
will be sparkling rooms that you will
enjoy living in.

my philosophy

Often, homes that are entirely professionally decorated do not clearly express their owners' personalities. If you are reading my book, you are probably not using a full-service decorator. Maybe you prefer to do the job yourself, or perhaps you haven't the budget for it. Maybe you aren't trying to achieve a "decorated" look. Regardless of whether you use professional decorating help or not, it is important to decorate your home so that it reveals your passions, collections, histories, hobbies, and other interests. Don't strive for perfection. A house that looks too perfect or overly decorated can prevent its occupants from feeling at home or using the things they live with, even in casually decorated rooms. This is because the objects seem to be there for display rather than for use. It looks as if no one really lives in such perfect rooms. Besides, it is impractical—especially if you have children or pets—and it is expensive. If you welcome imperfection into your home, people will feel more comfortable. Decide on the look you are after and then, as it is your home, present your personality and that of your family in your rooms.

When I choose furnishings and accessories, I assess them for their function, their aesthetic value, and their meaning to me. You can do the same. I appreciate the beauty and simplicity of handmade objects, even the humblest thing. Your child's plaster-cast handprint, for example, with its sentimental charm, can easily be integrated into a grouping of wall-hung photos, even in a formal decor. Identify objects that move you or are meaningful to you and integrate them with your rooms. Throughout this book, I talk about many ways to do this.

Explore your family's history as part of the decorating process. Ancestry can be compelling and fascinating. It enriches our lives. Our homes take on additional meaning when they reflect our origins. You might collect objects that relate to your cultural background or ethnicity. Perhaps you inherited treasured family heirlooms or photos that you want to feature in your home.

Your home need not be filled with expensive things to be beautiful or luxurious. Many of today's stores carry a wide range of deceptively expensive-looking furnishings and accessories that look handmade. You don't need to open your pocket very wide to achieve your desired result. Rather, you need to know what items of furniture to splurge on and where to use budget fill-ins. For instance, you might spring for a well-built, comfortable sofa and settle for inexpensive flea-market side tables. Use your instinct to choose home furnishings that reflect how you want to live, look, and feel in your space. *Perfect Palettes for Painting Rooms* does not seek perfection for designers but for you—the goal is the ideal room for your purposes.

Perfect Palettes for Painting Rooms is divided into two parts. Part 1: Basic Design Principles helps you think about the tone you want to set in your rooms and includes five detailed steps to decorating and accessorizing. Part 2: Rooms and Recipes is a collection of inspiring room themes that includes paint color palettes and photographs divided by room type. I've also included appendixes with additional details on room structure, color scheme, fabrics, windows, lighting, picture hanging, and the treatment of entryways and hallways for people who wish to take on the finer points of decorating.

REDECORATE

YOU CAN HIRE a decorator (some are called redecorators) for short-term assistance, even same-day makeovers, to get help with furniture arrangements, paint colors, lighting, and so on. This can be helpful to people who need a jump start or who are paralyzed by every little decorating decision, so consider it if you need to. Check the home section in your local newspaper or local city magazine for names.

your inspiration

The unique feature of this decorating book is its recipes. A recipe is a ready-made inspiration of possibility for decorating a room. Each room recipe has a title based on a theme or a notion and evokes a unique mood, style, flavor, or identity. Collectively, the recipes represent a wide range of decorating styles and tastes. I created these recipes with particular rooms in mind, but you can apply the theme of any recipe to any room. For example, Music Under the Stars was designed for a dining room, but you can use it in a bedroom if you prefer.

Perfect Palettes for Painting Rooms helps you find the best paint colors for your rooms. Even the white and off-white choices are wonderful! Use a recipe just as it appears in this book or alter it to your liking. You might choose to use your imagination to vary a recipe. Your recipe can replicate the mood and colors created by your favorite artist. If you are attracted to a particular country or culture, you may want to find ways to express that in your room.

Once you have selected a theme for a room, you can apply the decorating tips found throughout this book. Then you will be on your way to developing a truly personal living environment.

A theme can spill over gracefully from room to room. Adhering to a single theme throughout your home may give it a unified and consistent look, but by no means must you do so. Most of our homes have rooms decorated in different styles, and I encourage you to express your various moods and tastes. This often means including a variety of themes, furniture styles, and accessories in different rooms. Even a home with multiple themes, mix-and-match furniture, and multicolored rooms can look unified if you build on the colors of your furnishings and accessories. This is one of the simplest ways to unify the rooms in your home (see appendixes A and B). Emphasize continuity between rooms by using the same degree of formality or casualness throughout the house. To understand the making of formal and casual spaces, read chapter 1. Rest assured that if you follow even some of the guidelines in this book, the look of your rooms will improve.

style

Over the last decade, decorating definitions have become more flexible. The line dividing formal from casual has become less distinct. Chosen carefully, a rusty iron gate covered with a sheet of glass can serve as a coffee-table top in a formal living room or as a casual table in a cozy family room. This is great news for all of us with a mixture of furnishings.

While decorating styles have become more loosely defined, professional decorators still prefer to divide them into categories: formal, traditional, casual, country, contemporary, eclectic, adventurous, retro, romantic, Victorian, and so on. Few people choose a style that falls exactly within the bounds of one of these decorating categories and suddenly know how to create that look. The recipes in this book eliminate the need for you to learn all there is to know about decorating styles. Instead, you will learn how to view styles of decorating as either casual, formal, or in between. The following brief descriptions may help you find where you fit before you read the detailed style information for each room type in part 2.

FORMAL

A sense of order characterizes a formal setting. This is usually achieved by symmetry. For formal balance, equally distribute objects of similar weight, size, and shape on each side of an imaginary line that goes through the middle of space, creating a mirror image. This applies to both the room as a whole and to smaller areas such as a fireplace mantel or china cabinet. Imagine a mantel with a pair of beautiful topiaries flanking a gilded mirror or painting. Formal style can be achieved with your existing furniture and art objects. Just place them in balanced positions in the room and in relation to each other. Whether using contemporary furniture, with its straightforward, clean lines, or traditional, antique, or more ornate furniture and accessories, it is the symmetrical, balanced placement of large and small objects that make a room feel formal.

If what you own is traditional, you can combine your matched sets of furniture in rich colors and highly polished finishes with luxurious, refined smooth fabrics. Include mementos that convey a sense of heritage, objects with classic forms, and a beauty rooted in tradition. When we think of formal decor, we think of a setting of luxury and grandness or one of gentility and grace. Often this is achieved with elegantly framed paintings and mirrors and with cornice moldings and other architectural ornamentation. Such a setting might include elaborate window treatments of plush fabrics with elegant braids, fringes, and rosettes.

If your home furnishings are contemporary, you may create a museumlike starkness that has an orderly, architectural beauty. Remarkably, a few objects made from diverse materials, when carefully placed in a contemporary room, can work well together despite their contrasts in texture, reflectivity, and color. Your furnishings, art, and accessories in leather, glass, metal, exotic wood, and even concrete or plaster can be integrated to create a chic, formal, contemporary space.

CASUAL

To make your room feel family friendly or to reflect a casual lifestyle without losing touch with classical elements, reduce the use of symmetry. Don't make things balance as mirror images; instead, allow some irregularity and leave some spaces blank. Introduce a casual fabric to soften hard-edged furniture with loose-fitting slipcovers. If not one cozy object is in a room you hope to make a bit more casual, add a soft, overstuffed piece like a rolled-arm sofa, an end-of-the-bed upholstered bench and throw blanket, or a tufted ottoman. Asymmetrically combining your formal furniture and accessories with comforting objects such as plants, rustic hewn pieces, or a pine coffee table, will instantly take the edge off the formality.

Casual decorating creates an inviting, put-your-feet-up atmosphere. Use all of your relaxed, comfortable, unfussy mix-and-match furniture, and arrange it mostly asymmetrically. In a room with a mantel, for example, you might display five objects on one side and balance them with a single, large piece on the other side. Balance is important, but mirror-image symmetry is not. Your whimsical and personal objects will suit casual room displays better than fragile heirloom items will. You can choose easy-care fabrics and floor coverings that are textured or nubby. Contrast textures, shapes, and design origins. Whether you love romantic, delicate pastel flowers and china or colorful and bold contemporary art, use those key concepts of balance and proportion throughout the room. Choose less-tailored window treatments, whether decorative shutters or fabric blinds. Windows may even be kept bare.

YOUR APPROACH

Do you take an adventuresome approach to decorating, believing the more, the better? Your beloved objects may be numerous, disparate, varied, and seemingly unrelated, but they needn't appear crammed or cluttered, and they needn't be relegated to the attic, either. Throughout this book, I describe innovative ways to make your eclectic collections work together by adhering to principles of balance and proportion.

Do you prefer a lean aesthetic: an orderly, highly functional, uncluttered space? Put only a few objects in the room. You may want to choose them chiefly for their form and function or because they are your favorites. Either way, carefully edit the displays to give a clean, open, simple look.

As you work to determine your own personal style, consider your lifestyle. Do you live in a city apartment, a sprawling house in the suburbs, or a cottage at the beach? Are you a homebody? Are you a neatnik or a more relaxed homemaker? Do you like to entertain, or is your place a private haven? Do you have children or pets?

How upset are you if a favorite object gets broken? I have small children, so I don't display precious accessories on my tabletops. I also removed our white carpet from the family room and replaced it with an oriental rug that hides a multitude of sins. Over the years, I have added and subtracted objects to reflect where I am in my life at the moment.

You can achieve the atmosphere you desire in a room with almost any kind of furniture. One of my Californian clients wanted a serene, contemporary, but feminine bedroom. Because her existing furniture was country in style, she feared she would have to buy all new furniture to achieve her goal, but she did not have the budget for it. We kept her country-style furniture and selected colors and accessories for the room from the recipe in this book called Coastal Dreams to create the room she wanted—a beautiful retreat. Once your furniture is in place, you can accessorize to convey a recipe's theme and create the atmosphere you desire.

decorating in five steps

1

CLEAR OUT THE ROOM

To get a better perspective on a room, I empty out some, if not all, of its contents, especially the accessories, such as artwork on the walls and objects covering the furniture's surfaces, and place the accessories in a holding area. Sometimes I even remove the furniture, but you don't have to. It always amazes me how much easier changing decor becomes when I take this approach. I strongly suggest you approach your room this way too. I then rearrange the furniture and add things back carefully and thoughtfully. The minute the objects begin to look unbalanced, I remove them again and stop. With this approach, your room will look fine at every stopping point until it is completed. I don't put objects in a room just to get it decorated or to use everything I have; that is a prescription for decorating confusion. If you decorate your rooms only by adding things, you will be disappointed with the results.

2

LOOK AT THE ROOM'S STRUCTURE

Consider the structure of the room itself: the floor, the ceiling, the walls. These elements can make a critical difference in the direction of your decor. Are your floors hardwood or carpeted, colored or neutral? Are your walls papered, painted, or paneled? Are your ceilings high, low, or mid-height? Which structural elements should be emphasized or minimized? Keep in mind that all the existing colors that you don't change must be factored into the new color scheme. You may choose to do nothing to the room's structure, to make only minor changes to your floors, ceiling, and walls, or to get deeply involved in treatments. For specific details on addressing your room's structure, turn to appendix A.

3

CHOOSE A RECIPE

Select a room in which to begin your decorating and accessorizing journey. Let's say it's the living room. Turn to the chapter on living rooms. Find a tranquil place and take some time to leaf through the recipes. Allow your eyes to move slowly over the pages and settle on a favorite. Notice that at the end of each recipe is a short list of accessory ideas. The items listed are meant to help you to get the room's theme established at the outset. Please be aware that I have suggested a style or theme (Asian style, French casual elegance, antique, and so on) for each recipe, but don't feel limited by these themes. They are a way to help people relate to the colors and get a sense of the mood each recipe evokes. The themes relate to the paint color palettes, but the color palettes can be used in any style of decor. Note that the color palettes include specific paint manufacturer color numbers. Use these colors or choose your own. (To use paint color palettes, see appendixes A and B.) Once you have your desired paint colors on your walls, it will much easier to accomplish your decorating goals.

4

DETERMINE THE FURNITURE PLACEMENT

You have cleared the room, addressed its structure, selected a recipe, and painted. Now you may put the furniture in place. For guidance, turn to the end of the chapter for that specific room. There you will find a description of the room's function, room-specific information on furniture and its placement, and guidelines on accessorizing the room.

Using the material provided, carefully consider how your family room functions, given your family's lifestyle. Look over your furniture and decide what to keep, add, or banish. Whether you are designing the room from scratch or rearranging what you already have, an inviting room often has less to do with its contents and more to do with how you use them. Thus, you must put the pieces in their "right" places. Consider also the guidelines below. These general guidelines for furniture placement can be applied to any room in your home.

To place your furniture, you will want to:

- Identify the room's focal point.
- Examine the scale of your furniture and then arrange it.

FOCAL POINT

A focal point is the most dramatic element within a room, its aesthetic center. The room's furniture arrangement is based on and around the focal point. Perhaps your living room or family room has a fireplace, a beautiful arched window with a view, a pair of French doors, or a wall of built-in bookshelves and cabinets. Once you've identified the focal point, emphasize it. If it is a fireplace, create a display on the mantel and flank the fireplace with topiaries, columns, or sconces. You can fill the inside of the fireplace with dried flowers and cut a mirror to fit.

If your room has no obvious focal point, create one. You can build a faux fireplace by attaching a fireplace surround to the wall. Your sofa can become the focal point if you hang a lovely, grand mirror above it for architectural interest. Any dramatic print or painting can serve this purpose. A large rug or another bold-colored or large-scale accessory will do the trick, as will a large piece of furniture, such as an armoire. An elegant chandelier can become the focal point of your dining room. Even a wall with a large arrangement of framed photos can be a room's focal point. In some rooms, however, such as the bedroom, the focal point will be defined by the function of the room. Your bed itself, or an interesting headboard, is almost always the focal point.

The focal point is the cornerstone of the furniture arrangement. If the room is large, it may have more than one focal point. Perhaps your living room has a beautiful bay window and a lovely fireplace. You can create two or more furniture groupings to reinforce both focal points.

SCALE OF FURNITURE

Consider the scale or proportion of your major pieces of furniture as well as their style and color. For example, your reed-thin chair may be the same height as your rolled-arm chair, but they have different visual weights. Notice how they look awkward together. Use the following tips to help with your furniture arrangement.

- Arrange your major pieces of furniture first. Work around the focal point.
- Balance your combination of large- and small-scale furniture. Avoid placing a tiny, delicate table next to a large, overstuffed couch—likewise, avoid a tiny lamp on a large side table. Your goal is to arrange the furniture so that it appears compatible in scale.
- Group your small furnishings together. On their own, small things tend to get lost.
- A single, large-scale piece, such as a couch, love seat, or armoire, makes even a small room feel larger. Large and small rooms both benefit from at least one piece of large-scale furniture.
- Equally distribute tall and weighty pieces on both sides of a room, not all on the same side. If you have only one tall piece, add another element to create height. A tall standing screen or artwork, sconces, or mirrors hung above a low piece of furniture give a sense of height.

- Short of buying new furniture, exploiting fabric coverings is the easiest way to balance the visual weight of the furniture in a room. For example, if you have spindly wooden chairs and a large, weighty couch, you can add skirted slipcovers to the chairs for instant visual weight.
- If you are a novice and nervous about mixing furniture styles, stick to furniture in neutral colors, such as wood, wicker, and white. They are easier to mix.
- Always zone for traffic, giving people enough space to maneuver around a room. Allow 3 to 4 feet (.9 to 1.2 meters) of clearance at the entrance. Walkways should be at least 30 inches (76 cm) wide.

Remember, most rooms have one or more inherent architectural limitations. They may have walls broken up by many windows or doors. They may appear or feel boxy or tunnel-like. Maybe they have awkward dormers. You can address all of these problems. Here are a few tips:

- If the room is long and narrow, help square it visually with a wide piece of furniture across one of the narrow ends. Try a wall of bookshelves or a long couch flanked by end tables.
- To alleviate a boxy look, try to float furniture groupings by moving the furniture away from the walls.
- Arranging the furniture on the diagonal widens the room visually and makes more room for seating.

- If you have an unused recessed area, such as a dormer window, try built-in bookshelves, a built-in desk, a window seat, or a bookcase the height of the sill.
- If multiple doorways interrupt the walls, paint the door frames, the doors, the wood trim, and the walls all the same color. This draws attention away from them.
- If the room has few or tiny windows, deflect the attention from them with simple window treatments. Create a focal point with your furnishings.
- If you can't disguise an architectural problem, draw attention away from it by creating a focal point elsewhere in the room.

5

PLACING THE ACCESSORIES

Your wall colors, flooring, and ceiling treatments are in place and the furniture is arranged. Now it is time to add personality and warmth. Put your unique and wonderful mark on your surroundings. To do this, use the recipe you have chosen and the following guidelines:

- Consider your decorating style preferences.
- Survey your accessories.
- Group accessories by shape, color, material, or theme.
- Display groupings.

DECORATING STYLE

You have already read the style guidelines presented earlier in this chapter. By adhering to your style preferences, you will achieve and maintain consistency throughout the room. It may help you to know that your accessorizing style is often a reflection of your style of dress. Your accessories become to your rooms what jewelry, scarves, jackets, hats, coats, and shoes are to your clothing. So, if you don't embellish your clothing much, you may have a more minimalist approach to accessorizing your rooms as well.

SURVEY ACCESSORIES

The surfaces are empty; the walls are painted. Accessories have been collected from all over the house and are in a holding area. Now take a look at the objects you have pulled together. While they are in a neutral context, view them with a fresh eye. Perhaps you have strong doubts about some items; if so, put them away for a while, or if you are sure you are ready to let go, toss them. Be sure to set all of your favorite things in one area. Starting with your favorites, begin to group your things according to the following guidelines but don't put them in the room yet.

GROUP ACCESSORIES

Grouping related objects gives each object greater impact than if it stood alone. Accessorizing depends on strength in numbers, and collections are desirable. Three or more of anything constitutes a collection. Collections can be a unifying element, whether they are the same color, made of similar material, or linked thematically. Grouping like objects doesn't mean they have to match. You could group vases of the same color but with different shapes and handles, or group blue and white china of different patterns. Check these tips for grouping objects:

- Group objects by color, shape, material, or theme.
- Pairing objects is a balanced way to group accessories, create symmetry, and develop a cohesive look. Pairs don't have to be identical; try pairing two different lamps of the same scale and colors.
- To increase their impact, cluster small items together. Small objects tend to get lost when displayed by themselves.
- If you have objects that relate to a theme, such as duck decoys or animal figurines, group them together. If you happen to have or can buy a print or poster with the same theme, hang or stand it nearby to reinforce the point.
- Group unlike things on a tray or in an open box to unify them.
- A large accessory can add punch to a dull room. Consider a large print, painting, or rug.
- Use an odd number of objects in your less formal or symmetric displays. An odd number has more visual appeal as a vignette (a grouping of objects).

- Display multiple objects of similar material (for example, chrome or brass) three or four times in the room. Repeating the similar material creates unity.

- For tabletop displays, choose items of various heights, short to tall. Some decorators suggest setting the largest item in the center with smaller pieces radiating from it. Others say to put the taller items in back and the smaller toward the front. This method is preferable for displays like a tabletop gallery of family photos. See which approach you find most appealing.

- To display items on a shelf, arrange them in a line or stagger them in a front-to-back pattern.

- To create quiet areas in your room, free those areas of objects. Not all parts of a room need dramatic impact.

- Display what you love; don't display everything you have.

- Leave breathing room between collections when you place them in the room.

- Accessories hung on the walls warm the room. Walls can benefit from the simplest poster, plates, quilt, hanging, or print. Wall art can even become the focal point of a seating group.

- If the walls are papered with a bold print, consider hanging simple, monochromatic pieces like mirrors or lithographs.

- A wide frame or large mat (the paper board inside the picture frame that acts as a border between art and frame) provides white space between wall and art.

DISPLAY GROUPINGS
Analyze the accessories and groupings you have been setting aside. Choose those that complement your recipe's theme and begin to display them in the room.

Good luck and have fun!

COLOR TIP

KEEP IN MIND that bold colors and lively patterns on your wall coverings, fabrics, rugs, and carpets have the most dramatic impact on your room but also require a little daring and skill, which you can acquire by reading appendixes B and C. However, if you are feeling timid, you may be wise to opt for simplicity. Begin with neutral colors and minimal patterns on your furnishings. Add interest and drama with textured rugs, textured fabrics, and other accessories. As you become comfortable with the decorating process, you can carefully add more colors and patterns, starting with small objects such as throw pillows, rugs, and afghans placed around the room for balance. Work your way up to bolder colors and patterns on upholstery, draperies, or slipcovers.

living rooms

**THE LIVING ROOM'S
FUNCTION AND STYLE**

The living room is often defined by how it looks, not how comfortable or functional it is. The room may be off limits except as a meeting place for guests and entertaining. It is often the hands-off-or-else room. Paradoxically, it may be the largest room in the house. Your living room is what you make of it. It can be versatile and serve as a favorite place to spend time with your family relaxing, reading, and socializing as well as a place to entertain. It can double as a family room, a library, a music room, or a home office. It can be a showplace used mainly for special occasions and guests.

Is the look of your living room as important, or more or less important, than comfort or function? Do you entertain a few friends or business associates at a time, or larger groups? Do you entertain formally?

Answering questions like these about the function of your living room will guide you in decorating it. Your choice of a decorating style will also be based on your personal needs and priorities. We all have varied lifestyles; use your own as a point of departure in decorating.

It's not houses that I love, it's the life I live in them.

—GABRIELLE "COCO" CHANEL, FASHION DESIGNER

moderne

My inspiration for this color scheme came from an interest in tribal art and the Jazz Modern style of the 1920s. Geometric motifs derived from many sources, including the tomb of Tutankhamen, which was discovered in 1921, were combined with bold, often clashing colors. A visually exhilarating room is the result.

This is a place where you can display both your fragile objects and more solidly built art objects. Freely display collectibles, such as Italian blown glass and pottery. Put antique or contemporary stemware in a curio cabinet. Hang contemporary posters framed in chrome, black, or wood.

An eclectic mix of furniture and accessories with simple lines can be loaded with texture and subtle color. Wood finishes, steel, and even plastic furniture and accessories all work together. For fabrics, use abstract prints as well as solids. Objects from different periods and styles can complement each other, like Navajo rugs and tribal vessels. Brightly colored earth tones, such as reds and ocher, warm the space. Pull out collectibles gathered on your travels and see whether or not you can use them. Make your own statement, but remember to use color as the unifying element in the room (see appendix B). This room will truly represent you, your past and present. Store objects that you want out of the way in an old trunk set in a corner, in baskets, or even in metal boxes. Sink into a buttery leather or faux leather chair.

Your love for company can be expressed by having this living room double as guest room for overnight guests. Pile oversize pillows on the floor. The key is to make the room as enjoyable and pleasant as the room where you put your feet up at night.

All music is folk music. I ain't never heard no horse sing a song.

—LOUIS ARMSTRONG

Metropolitan, adult, sophisticated

WALLS
Benjamin Moore Blue Lapis #2067-40

TRIM
Benjamin Moore Atrium White

ACCENTS
Red, Yellow

ACCESSORY IDEAS
- Framed poster(s)
- Jewel-toned art objects
- Tribal art
- Colorful Oriental rug(s)
- Glass and pottery collections

Casual elegance, minimal, bright

WALLS
Sherwin-Williams Yellow Banana
SW 1663

TRIM
Sherwin-Williams Natural Silk
SW 1662

ACCENTS
Red, Coral

ACCESSORY IDEAS
○ Willow branches
○ Plantation shutters
○ Contemporary floor lamps
○ Floral chain-stitched rug

springtime

Even as a small child, I knew that red and yellow tulips confirmed the arrival of spring. This was my inspiration for this Springtime living room. Think of early, warm spring breezes and colors borrowed from butterfly wings, like sunny citrine yellow. Take delight in your sparkling living room.

Keep the walls bright. If you don't have hardwood floors, consider wall-to-wall carpeting the color of straw, or add hushed color in a lovely chain-stitched or floral hand-hooked rug. Interesting floor lamps eliminate the need for multiple tables with side lamps, maintaining a sparse, fresh, clean, springlike atmosphere.

Use natural wood furniture with sleek lines, and sprinkle in a few lovely antiques, if you have them. Store all paraphernalia. Tree branches make a stark but striking display. Window treatments are unusual and appealing, adding a sophisticated twist—casual plantation shutters on one window and formal drapes on another.

It's springtime all year round in this lovely living room.

For brilliant plants to charm the eye, What plant can with the tulip vie?

—ANONYMOUS

okavango

One of the most splendid and unexpected wonders in the world is in southern Africa. It is an unspoiled gem—water in the desert, specifically a layer of water known as the Okavango that stretches over 8,500 square miles (22,015 square kilometers) of the Kalahari Desert. Imagine the wonder of it—the largest inland delta in the world—and the life it supports. It is a water wilderness of green papyrus and glorious blue water and sky. Elephants, lions, giraffes, hippos, crocodiles, and a host of other free-roaming wildlife remain unharrassed in Okavango.

Choose earthy and grounding colors for the background—walls, floor, and largest furnishings—in red, gold, straw, sand, black, brown, or green. Picture your living room as an open space containing few furnishings, with exotic, carefully selected surprises placed throughout. Wall coverings or accents that look like woven grasses complement masks or carvings in ebony and exotic woods. Traditional African fabrics, batiks, and kilims, can be fashioned into pillows, runners, or table covers. A splash of animal print provides contrast on a pillow or area rug. Use these different patterns generously. Add an occasional exuberantly bright accent in sizzling yellow or orange. Emphasize texture with sturdy wicker furniture, sisal carpet, or rugs in tan or ivory. Accessorize with baskets, tribal stools that double as small tables, houseplants, and one-of-a-kind cultural elements. For an interesting twist, mount antlers on the wall. Display tribal art. On windows, use anything from matchstick shades to simple filmy fabrics, or combine treatments.

There is always something new out of Africa.

—GREEK PROVERB

Earthy, adventuresome

WALLS
Laura Ashley Raspberry #5392 964

TRIM
Natural wood or main color

ACCENTS
Gold

ACCESSORY IDEAS
- Tribal art
- African landscape prints
- Animal statuary or figurines
- Animal print or native African fabrics
- Houseplants and baskets
- African tribal stools

Formal, elegant

WALLS
Benjamin Moore White Sand OC-10

TRIM
Benjamin Moore Brilliant White

ACCESSORY IDEAS
- Pillows in delicate colors
- Simply framed prints and paintings (florals, reproductions of the masters, portraiture)
- Neutral rug(s) in muted colors

swan lake

On a brilliant, beautiful spring day, walk through flower gardens at a local park—or a place like the duck pond at the Boston Public Garden, where swans are released each May. Beneath the delicate new foliage, watch these birds swimming, graceful and elegant. It is compelling and heartwarming to learn that swans mate for life.

Remember the sweet story of the ugly ducking who as a gosling is teased and humiliated, then grows up to realize he is actually a beautiful swan? Interestingly, the first performance of Tchaikovsky's ballet *Swan Lake* was a disaster, an ugly duckling itself. It achieved success only after Tchaikovsky's death in 1893 and became the first ballet to raise the dance form to the level of serious theater. The ballet is glorious to watch.

Think of springtime, with its fragrant lilacs, lily of the valley, and Easter lilies. Use a white color palette. White conveys inno-cence and purity. For many people, white paint is the color of choice for every room in the house because it is safe. But, this recipe incorporates multiple whites for an interesting and beau-tiful affect. These whites range from a slightly warm, gray, and off-white on the walls to a pure white on the ceiling, and a slightly creamier, rich white on the trim (moldings, wainscoting, window trim, doors). In an area as minimal and sleek as this one, pure white on the walls would create glare and cause after-image. It would be downright inhospitable. But whiter whites work well on trim, giving it a crisp and finished look that help to define the space.

White, like the swan, predominates in this monochromatic room on furniture as well. Choose white lamps and neutral accessories, like this wheat-colored rug. Delicate floral prints on pillows add the only hint of color in the room.

A swan is breasting the flow all in himself
enfolded, a slow-moving tableau.

—PAUL HINDEMITH

Bright, fun, lively

tangerine and pear

Our five senses need nourishment, so why can't your living room serve the senses with a treasure trove of color, texture, and design? Be a little flamboyant and bring positive changes to your attitude with sumptuous tangerine orange walls that fill the atmosphere with warmth, charm, and fun. These colors of garden-fresh fruit are not only visually stimulating, but they also lift your spirits and relieve the pressures of the day.

The furniture for this bright color scheme has simple lines and is relaxed and amusing. The outcome is a versatile room that can do triple duty as a living room, family room, and playroom. It's practical, comfortable, and beautifully balanced. Nothing here is too precious to be enjoyed.

Have fun with print pillows, keeping red, pear green, and tangerine orange the main colors. Accent colors are neutral golden wheat and wood tones. Include unique items, such as this amazing array of contemporary standing lamps, geometric painted vases, and colorful boxes. Paint an old door with chalkboard paint to create a large drawing surface for the kids. Have plants near you. Keep the windows bare to flood the room with light.

This room is absolutely alive. It influences one's sense of well-being and satisfaction. In addition, guests will never cease to be surprised by the joy of this unexpected color.

WALLS
Glidden Carotene #97YR 44/642

ACCENTS
Brown, Green

ACCESSORY IDEAS
◦ Brightly printed pillows
◦ Contemporary lamps
◦ Geometric pottery pieces
◦ Chrome-legged chairs
◦ Stacking storage boxes

Life is a banquet and most poor suckers are starving to death.

—AUNTIE MAME

Country craftsmanship

WALLS
Glidden Express Blue #70BB 16/287

TRIM
Glidden Egret

ACCENTS
Red, Yellow

ACCESSORY IDEAS
- Old quilts
- Needlepoint or tapestry framed and hung on the wall
- Handcrafted rugs and blankets
- Metalwork and glass objects

arts and crafts

Growing up should be an experience filled with art. Many families spend time together by sharing interests such as basketry, printmaking, ceramics, hooked rugs, embroidery, knitting, quilting, and sewing. People often believe that handmade creations such as quilts and pottery are better than anything you can buy. The Arts and Crafts movement began as a rebellion against mechanization and mass production in Victorian England, and focused on high-quality, handcrafted items.

In a living room in this style, use as many handcrafted items as possible. Include at least one piece of large-scale furniture. Use well-constructed, aesthetically pleasing, perhaps exotic wood furniture. Craftsmanship characterizes the style. Incorporate metalwork and glass objects, handwoven blankets, and hand-hooked rugs or quilts. Paint walls in daring color. Create an instant tapestry by suspending a fabric remnant from a wall-hung rod. Interesting stone or ceramic tile is wonderful on floors. Framed needlework, needlepoint pillows, colorful rugs, hand-painted ceramics, antiques of all kinds, stained-glass window panels, a bowl of fragrant flowers, turned wood candlesticks, and painted landscapes finish off the room.

Have nothing in your houses that you do not know to be useful, or believe to be beautiful.

—WILLIAM MORRIS

feed the birds

When it comes to backyard birding, some folks have more luck attracting squirrels to their feeders. However, with the installation of a truly squirrel-baffling feeder and a more careful selection of bird food, you'll have no trouble drawing hundreds of birds your way all year long. Doves, cardinals, robins, house finches, woodpeckers, goldfinches, and even bluebirds may stop by. It's interesting to note, as you sit and watch them, that their patches of color often send signals to other birds of the same species. For instance, the male robin's red breast lets other males know that this territory is taken.

This living room reflects a love of nature and backyard birding. Like every room in the home, it provides more than just function and beauty. It nourishes an interest. It reflects the inhabitants of the house. In this room, I almost feel as if I'm outdoors. It's the way I feel relaxing on a beautiful, warm, breezy summer day—calm and restful. Pale, solid furniture provides a muted and low-key background. Use a casual cotton sheer or linen for window treatments. Select a rug that reinforces the room's color scheme. Enhance the atmosphere with prints of flowers and plenty of scented candles. Arrange pottery on shelves or tables. Display favorite artwork that ties in with the nature theme, such as these decorative birds. Painted trays, lamps, and decorative bowls contribute to the charm. Keep the mood light and airy. As you tinker, listen again to the beautiful song from *Mary Poppins* called "Feed the Birds."

No bird soars too high, if he soars with his own wings.

—WILLIAM BLAKE

Bright, sunny, country casual

WALLS
California Paints Phoenix Sun #7374D

TRIM
California Paints Floral White

ACCENTS
Red, Yellow

ACCESSORY IDEAS
- Prints of flowers or dried flowers or wreath
- Nature-related paintings or prints
- Birdhouses
- Carved wooden birds
- Ceramics

Colorful, exotic, adventurous

WALLS
Sherwin-Williams Willow #SW 1416

TRIM
Sherwin-Williams Natural Silk

ACCENTS
Gold, Red

ACCESSORY IDEAS
- Painted wicker or bamboo pieces
- Bright and/or tropical multicolored fabrics
- Framed prints of flowers
- Exotic flowers
- Palm plant

bird-of-paradise

The colors in this stunning room remind me of those in the exotic tropical bird-of-paradise flower—orange, red, and chartreuse. The color scheme evokes heat and adventure.

The bird-of-paradise plant is native to South Africa. Its stunning blossoms are pollinated not by bees but by sun birds and songbirds. Its bright blossoms and angular shape inspire this colorful style of decoration.

A hot, colorful theme is great in the living room. Along with bright upholstered furniture, choose red and orange painted pieces, like storage chests, side tables, even wicker lamps. Use loud stripes, multicolored fabric prints in tropical motifs, or more traditional fabrics such as damask (in bright colors) on your window treatments, or use matchstick roller shades or plantation shutters. Frame prints of tropical flowers. Keep fresh flowers, like the bird-of-paradise, in a tall, colorful vase. Consider nurturing a large palm plant for greenery. Introduce the orange and red of tropical blossoms in pillar candles and other accessories.

If contemporary decor is your style, keep it streamlined and minimal. Hang prints in a Peter Max style—multicolored and modern—framed in black, red, or white. A hand-painted piece of furniture in bold designs and colors with lots of contrast contributes a delightful bit of whimsy. Uncover hardwood floors, or choose carpet in a neutral wool Berber.

Take a walk on the wild side.

—LOU REED

The title of "Russian painter" means more to me than any international fame.... In my paintings there is not one centimeter that is free from nostalgia for my native land.

—MARC CHAGALL

chagall

This radiant, lively theme is reminiscent of the paintings of Marc Chagall, who was inspired, in large part, by Jewish and Russian folklore. His paintings often convey joy, tenderness, and peace, and almost always combine fantasy with reality. His work has a delightful, magical quality; this is the feeling you will create in your room. The themes and colors of his paintings can serve as your starting point. To get into the mood, look at a book of Chagall's paintings at the library or bookstore. A few favorites are *Le Soir à la Fenêtre* (*Evening at the Window*) and *La Fiancée au Visage Bleu* (*Bride with Blue Face*).

Notice the generous use of color on the accessories in this bright and airy yellow room. Imagine a comfortable, eclectic combination of furnishings and accessories in your space. Mix your old Naugahyde chairs with newer furnishings. Include a cushy couch in solid brushed cotton, corduroy, or chenille; this will add to the restful feeling. Introduce pattern on rugs and throw pillows.

Add a sense of surprise and fantasy by distributing whimsical objects in corners and atop shelves. These could include carved wooden figurines of people or animals (like Chagall's roosters), musical instruments (the violin, in particular, appears often in Chagall's paintings), an aquarium full of fish, a hanging mobile, metalwork candlesticks, colored glass objects, or patterned ceramics. Display your favorite collection. Haven't got any collections? Buying folk art objects at import stores is an inexpensive way to form an instant collection. Arts and crafts galleries carry whirligigs, kaleidoscopes, and mobiles. Hang colorful prints and paintings on walls, like Chagall reproductions. Include at least one vase packed with flowers, real or silk.

Eclectic, whimsical, relaxed

WALLS
California Paints Warm Rays #7262

TRIM
California Paints Floral White

ACCENTS
Red, Blue

ACCESSORY IDEAS
- Grouping of Chagall prints or other artists' prints
- Collection of folk art objects, such as carved wooden animals
- Ceramic or glass vessels in bold, colorful patterns or primary colors
- Colorful mobile

living room furniture

CORE FURNITURE

- couch or love seat(s)
- one or two comfortable (upholstered) chairs
- coffee table
- side table(s)
- storage units (armoire, built-in cabinets, bookshelves)

Examine your furniture. How many core pieces do you have? These pieces are essential. Will you be including additional furniture in your living room? For example, a desk or secretary, an armoire that contains your computer or entertainment center, a piano, or perhaps a chair and table for a reading nook. Remember, one or two oversized pieces of furniture, like a tall armoire, make even a diminutive room look larger. It is far more attractive to use several large pieces than to squeeze a lot of small, spindly chairs and multiple accessories into a room.

Does your living room offer a single focal point like a fireplace, built-in bookcases, an entertainment center, or an expansive window—or more than one? Will you need to create your own focal point? If you have a large living room, you don't need to turn it into one large sitting area. Create several conversation areas facing several focal points. (See information on focal points on page 20.) The most inviting living rooms have appropriately placed, comfortable furniture arranged in conversation areas. People can sit facing each other and need not raise their voices to be heard.

A conversation area requires an upholstered couch or love seat, two upholstered or otherwise comfortable chairs, a coffee table large enough for books, magazines, and decorative objects like a vase of flowers, and one or two side tables. The coffee table is the centerpiece of the conversation area, and everyone should be within reasonable reach of it. You may also want to add a sofa table behind the couch.

An example of a conversation area arrangement is two chairs flanking and facing the couch with a coffee table between, creating a U-shape. A rug beneath defines the area. Such conversation areas or clusters face the focal point(s). A successful conversation area promotes comfort and allows traffic to flow freely in and out of the room without weaving between pieces of furniture.

When arranging your furniture, start with the largest piece of your core furniture (usually the couch), then add smaller pieces.

MAXIMIZE A SMALL living room with a large-scale piece, like an armoire or an oversized love seat (sleeper sofas come in love seat sizes if your living room does double duty as a guest room). This will give the room a feeling of grandeur.

THE COFFEE TABLE in a small room should be about 24 to 36 inches (61 cm to 91 cm). Consider one with a glass top, which consumes less visual space.

LINE A WALL with ready-to-assemble bookcases or custom built-ins. This makes the room seem larger by playing up vertical and horizontal lines.

USE AN OVERSIZED ottoman and chair instead of two chairs.

EMPLOY LIGHT FABRIC upholstery, walls, and window treatments.

PLACE A SOFA crosswise to emphasize the width of a narrow room rather than the length.

Living Room Furniture Arranging and Tips

- When purchasing a new sofa, invest in a good-quality piece. Use budget fill-ins elsewhere in the room.

- Chairs and sofas should be approximately the same height for balance—ideally, no more than a 5-inch difference in height when measured from the floor. Therefore, place higher wing-back chairs in their own conversational grouping.

- Use either all rounded, curved-arm upholstered pieces of furniture, or all square-line, straight-arm furniture. Mixing the two looks awkward.

- Consider moving the couch and chairs away from walls to facilitate conversation and coziness and to improve traffic flow.

- For an interesting look, place the sofa or love seat on the diagonal in a corner of the room, then set a table and lamp, a floor plant, or a screen behind it.

- Use soft, cushy pillows made of your favorite fabrics rather than the pillows that came with your sofa or love seat.

- Be sure that every seat has access to adequate reading light and a surface where drinks can be set down.

- Ottomans can do double duty as a side table or coffee table and as movable seating.

- Round skirted tables make great end tables. They are made of particleboard and are available at department stores. Cover with a beautiful fabric and add a ½-inch (.5 cm) thick glass top or mirror glass.

- Two small square tables set side by side can serve as a formal coffee table, as can a low chest.

- If the couch and chairs are light-weight, use end tables to provide weight—for example, small chests with drawers or shelves.

- End tables should be no more than 2 ½ inches (6 cm) higher or lower than the arms of the sofa or chairs.

- Examine the traffic patterns for entering and exiting the room. Set furniture at least 18 inches (46 cm) away from open doorways.

- To give character to the room, include at least one old or antique piece of furniture.

SOLVE STORAGE PROBLEMS with a well-designed media wall. Choose from a variety of possibilities for electronic equipment (TV, video or DVD player, CD player):

- lineup of ready-made modular storage units
- shelving and open or closed cabinets
- a closet with bifold doors and shelving
- a cabinet with doors for an uncluttered look
- an armoire with matching shelf units on each side for books and collections
- an angled cupboard with or without doors for TV, books, games, and videos
- bookshelves with standard louvered doors
- built-in units

KEEP CLUTTER INSIDE wall units and storage furniture.

Living Room Accessorizing Tips

- You may want to sketch a floor plan of your living room. Note the length and width of the room as well as the location of electrical outlets and windows. Where are the doorways? Evaluate your conversation area with respect to entering and exiting traffic and whether or not it faces a focal point.

- Reading lamps should measure from 26 to 30 inches (66 to 76 cm) high depending on the height of the end table. In general, the lower the table, the taller the lamp. For formal balance, it is best to use a pair of table lamps.

- Update older lamps with new shades.

- Revive old chairs and couches and pillows with slipcovers.

- Slipcovers look good on fully upholstered pieces, not wood-armed furniture. They can be fitted or slightly loose.

- Use area rugs to anchor furniture groupings.

- The largest area rug size for a living room is 3 feet (.9 meters) less than the width and 3 feet (.9 meters) less than the length of the room.

- Install picture lights over your favorite paintings for added atmosphere and an air of formality.

- In a large room, hang a fancy mirror on the wall so it is angled down to reflect the furniture. This creates more intimacy within the conversation area.

- Hang three or more ledges on the wall, like shelves, to hold your treasured artwork and favorite objects.

- Display a favorite object on a single decorative ornamental bracket, or hang a collection of them.

- Hang silhouettes of your kids and even your pets to personalize the space.

- A matted and framed vintage photo of your town, or a postcard about it, adds personality.

- A table gallery of family photos personalizes a tabletop or piano. Either use frames of all kinds or mix two or three of the same material, such as silver and gold leaf.

- Replace a modern fireplace mantel with an old one for added character.

- Vary the height of objects displayed on a mantel.

dining rooms

THE DINING ROOM'S FUNCTION AND STYLE

Whether you choose to have a dining room that is formal (and perhaps rarely used) or more casual (and perhaps frequently used), it should be comfortable and promote socializing.

Many of us spend time in the dining room at a variety of tasks besides eating. We wrap gifts, write letters or cards, do homework, work on the family photo album, and piece puzzles together. In my house, the sewing machine often rests on the dining room table, especially around holidays such as Halloween.

How do you use your dining room? Is it an integral part of your daily life? Is the dining table the first place you toss your keys, purse, and mail as soon as you come through the door, or is it a place reserved primarily for special occasions such as Thanksgiving feasts, birthday parties, and intimate formal dinners with company? How many people do you typically need to seat? Do you ever serve afternoon tea in your dining room? What about the style of the room? Rest assured that you can use your current furniture ensemble and modify it to move from casual to formal and vice versa.

Each recipe in this chapter provides the information you will need to create a particular style in your dining room. Your guests will always be more comfortable when you are comfortable, so choose the style that feels right for you. Even if you prefer a farmhouse or cottage-style dining room, the room will still be appropriate for anything from a splendid holiday feast to a light snack. I favor an eclectic approach that mixes formal touches with casual furnishings. However, if you love to dress to dine, you may prefer an altogether more formal, elegant dining room.

If you determine the function and the style of your dining room before you decorate it, the process will be much easier.

Life itself is the proper binge.

—JULIA CHILD

An old, old sight, and yet somehow so young; aye, and not changed a wink since I first saw it, a boy, from the hills of Nantucket! The same!—The Same!

—HERMAN MELVILLE, *MOBY DICK*

seaside home

Nantucket is an enchanting little jewel of an island off the coast of Massachusetts. Hundreds of authentic eighteenth-and nineteenth-century homes with exquisite architecture line its cobblestone streets. There are beautiful old-fashioned gardens everywhere. These remain from the whaling era, which brought great wealth to the island.

Lovely old seaside homes like this one abound in this little piece of paradise. The cinnamon and brown colors in this warm, rich dining room are appropriate to the home's era and are reminiscent of the colors of autumn. The room is serene, slow, soft, and quiet. Keep colors subdued, with little contrast.

Simple antique or reproduction Shaker-style furniture characterizes this room. Neutral-colored and minimalist accessories are offset by brighter color only on the tabletop. Otherwise the understated neutrality is maintained. Here, we see a rather casual eating area, but the recipe can be either formal or casual depending on your own touches. Nantucket baskets are beautiful in wheat tones. Fill one with willow branches, pussy willows, or dried bittersweet. Stick with an old-fashioned look. Think English countryside or cottage style. Dark or light wood tones both work. Even your most beat up, scratched, or weathered wooden furniture fits in this New England decor. Use violet and green accents on a table runner. A textured but neutral rug anchors your furniture grouping. Use a pale neutral Berber, a sisal rug, or a painted floor cloth. Display a trio of beeswax candles. Hang sailing ship and lighthouse prints, a kaleidoscope that looks like a ship's telescope, old bottles, weathervanes, scented candles in hurricane lamps, and painted boxes. Mount a barometer and thermometer on the wall. Include your shells, scrimshaw, weathered pebbles, scoured driftwood, cork, and sea glass. Frame and hang pictures of maritime scenes or nautical charts.

If you visit Nantucket, consider doing it in the autumn after the tourists have gone. Like the landscape in Scotland or Ireland, the vast marshland and moors are shades of red. There are many hiking trails through them. Purple aster and goldenrod grow profusely, as do highbush blueberry. The deep blue ocean surrounds it all. In October, the cranberry bogs are flooded to release the berries from the vines.

Perhaps you will catch a glimpse of the rising harvest moon on your next autumn visit to Nantucket.

DINING ROOM RECIPE

Serene, warm, restful

WALLS
Benjamin Moore Salmon Stream #2173-30

TRIM
Benjamin Moore Brilliant White

ACCENTS
Wood Tones

ACCESSORY IDEAS
- Pewter candlesticks
- Wooden bowls
- Hand-woven cotton table linens
- Shells and sea glass
- Pussy willow and dried bittersweet branches

Turn-of-the-century style, charming, inviting

WALLS
Benjamin Moore Confederate Red
#2080-20

TRIM
Benjamin Moore Acadia White

ACCENTS
Blue, Green, Yellow

ACCESSORY IDEAS
- Blue-and-white china collection
- Hooked or Oriental rug
- Antique or reproduction chandelier
- Elegant oil paintings or reproductions
- Silver (or plate) tea service
- Set of matching topiaries
- Silver wall sconces
- Antique or reproduction furniture

music under the stars

Imagine miles and miles of rolling green hills and seemingly endless natural beauty as a summer concert venue—a pastoral setting serving as a cultural mecca where world-class musicians perform. Glorious summer evenings filled with music!

Tanglewood, in the Berkshire Mountains of Massachusetts, is one such place. Visitors can stay in the neighboring village of Stockbridge. Main Street in this quaint town, where the painter Norman Rockwell lived, is lined with adorable antique buildings. The atmosphere is calming and relaxing. The mountain air, charming little pathways, gardens, and foliage all make this place picture postcard–perfect, just as in Rockwell's paintings.

This ideal combination of concepts and the antique furnishings like those at the local Red Lion Inn creates the mood in your dining room: charming, comfortable, beautiful, and historic. Soften the edges of the modern world by filling a curio cabinet with teacups and saucers. Display a soup tureen or an elegant flower arrangement on the buffet or in the center of the dining table. Place a tapestry runner on the table, or consider tapestry upholstery on chair seats. Your lighting, whether a crystal chandelier or porcelain table lamps, will cast a warm glow over treasured keepsakes. Wall sconces may flank a false fireplace or be mounted on either side of a lovely oil painting of a beloved ancestor. Make the dining area feel even more like the early 1900s with a chair rail and decorative molding. Incorporate elegant draperies if you wish. Display your antique or reproduction china and crystal collection. Add warmth and color by placing an Oriental rug beneath the dining table.

I kissed my first woman and smoked my first cigarette on the same day. I have never had time for tobacco since.

—ARTURO TOSCANINI

Casual, elegant

elegant
camp style

This room reflects your love of the outdoors and all the good times you have had fishing, boating, hiking, and swimming. It is cozy and natural, focused on the relaxed life.

Elegant camp style works as well in city dwellings as it does in country homes. Use woodsy materials like pine, oak, cedar, and twigs for furniture, paint your furniture white, or mix smooth stripped bark or twigs and the rough bark of the Adirondack style. This room is a good place for heavy old sideboards and dining tables with distressed finish as well as newer reproductions of old styles of furniture.

A generous use of wrought iron is found on many objects, including lamps and hardware. Mass together decorative objects, including ceramic bowls, carved wooden fish and birds, and vintage sporting and fishing reels. Mix in an unlikely contemporary print for your wall framed in simple black to add sophistication to the camp look.

Keep fabrics and table coverings simple in order to express an elegant simplicity. Spend hours at your dining table on rainy days doing puzzles or playing games like pick-up-sticks and Scrabble. Surround yourself in the colors of the natural forest.

True camp-style fans should visit the Adirondack Museum in Blue Mountain Lake, New York, where a rustic furniture fair and antique show is held every September.

WALLS
Benjamin Moore Green Grove
#2138-20

TRIM
Benjamin Moore Simple White

ACCENTS
Silver, Blue

ACCESSORY IDEAS
◦ Primitive ceramic bowls and plates
◦ Carved wooden fish and birds
◦ Wrought iron lamps and hardware
◦ Contemporary prints

The wilderness provides that perfect relaxation which all jaded minds require.

—WILLIAM H. H. MURRAY

Fun, colorful, inspiring

artist's house

Picture a woman at a loom in front of a window, or a man at a drawing table. The sun promises to chase the morning fog off the bay beyond.

In this space, art and design magazines are piled in the corner, and lovely artful surprises are scattered all around. The space is full of things, yet each has its place. Visitors to this space are drawn to the unusual color, the objects, and the different textures. They enjoy admiring the artwork and the many projects in progress while settling on a director's chair to nosh and chat.

This recipe was written for a dining room, but you may wish to try it in a home office or extra bedroom or adapt it for a teenager's bedroom or unfinished basement room. Strategically placed track lighting and task lighting allows you to create a studiolike feel (see appendix C).

Pull out those unfinished watercolors and needlepoint projects and display them. Unframed canvases, posters mounted behind glass, and paper sketches convey an arty look. Splash the walls with unusually bright color. This is a place to express yourself through art.

WALLS:
Pittsburgh Paints Golden Yarrow #211-5

TRIM
Pittsburgh Paints Silver Feather

ACCENTS
Violet, Blue

ACCESSORY IDEAS
- Art objects: sculpture, ceramics, glassware
- Posters, sketches, unframed artwork

What better way to spend one's life than to have as one's primary task the insistence on integrity of feeling. No wonder others are fascinated by artists.

—ROBERT MOTHERWELL

cassis

This lovely dining room features not only elegant furnishings but also rich purple walls inspired by the dark purple liqueur made from black currants, called cassis. What a marvelous atmosphere for wining and dining.

Traditional decor dominates, expressing a strong sense of hearth and home. Grace your home with antique or reproduction furniture in Chippendale, Queen Anne, Hitchcock, early American, or Shaker style, or a combination of these. Window treatments can be luxurious and flowing. Oriental rugs are the perfect floor covering in this room.

A wooden dining table, china chest, and sideboard in any of the above styles, or even reproductions from imported-furniture stores or used furniture shops, along with comfortable but elegant period chairs and, perhaps, several wing-back chairs banished from the living room are just right for this room. Antique-style lighting in crystal, pewter, brass, or silver complements the furniture. Accent the walls with traditional paintings, framed mirrors, or perhaps a family photo gallery.

Enter this room, and you can almost smell the aroma of sweet black currants.

The divine man dwells amidst gardens and orchards, a grower of plants and fruits.

—BRONSON ALCOTT

Traditional, down-to-earth antique style

WALLS
California Paints Salina Grape #7474D

TRIM
Benjamin Moore Atrium White

ACCENTS
Red/brown, Violet

ACCESSORY IDEAS
- Oriental-style rug
- Traditional china
- Antique or reproduction curtain tiebacks
- Antique or reproduction chandelier
- Formal drapes

Sophisticated country modern,
weathered

WALLS
Sherwin-Williams Yellow Warbler
#SW 1670

TRIM
Sherwin-Williams White Organdy

ACCENTS
Black, Green

ACCESSORY IDEAS
- Stars-and-Stripes motif on antique
  framed flags
- Framed embroidered sampler
- Earthenware pottery
- Carved decoys
- Antique clock
- Baskets

country modern

This dining room is pleasingly imperfect, yet its formal
symmetry gives it a modern bent. Whether in a Cape Cod beach
home or a log cabin in the Rockies, you can create a fresh
country modern look with the weatherbeaten beauty of the old
reconditioned with fresh paint—yellow, black, and white. Hang
a gilt-framed mirror and a hand-embroidered sampler on the
wall. If you have an interesting collection of artifacts, such as
these Native American arrowheads, frame and display them.
Include simple wooden chairs or a bench. To keep the look
sophisticated, avoid patterned fabrics such as stripes and
plaids. For an air of stark formality, employ plant stands such
as these to flank a mirror, fireplace, sideboard, or window.
Cattails make the perfect cut plant for display in tall vases.
Leave windows bare. Hang framed antique flag prints to
drive home the Stars-and-Stripes theme. Exhibit earthenware
pottery and carved decoys as well as Indian baskets. Include
an old clock.

For American antiques from 1700 to 1850, visit the annual
New York Winter Antiques Show and Americana auctions in
New York City.

The man on the railroad
track layin' crossties—
every time they hit the
hammer it was with a sad
feelin', but with a beat.

—MAHALIA JACKSON

dining room furniture

CORE FURNITURE

- dining room table and chairs
- sideboard or console table
- china chest or hutch

If you don't already have dining room furniture, buy your table first to conform to the shape and size of the room. Using the tips in this chapter, decide on round, square, rectangular, or oval. You need at least 8 square feet (2.4 meters) of floor space for a table for four, plus another 3 feet (.9 meters) in which to pull chairs in and out. Does your table have legs, a pedestal, or a trestle? Bear this aspect in mind as you decide whether to use chairs, with or without arms, upholstered chairs, or benches. You want to be sure your chairs will fit easily under the table. Place the table such that people can easily enter and exit the room, and keep the doorways free and clear for bringing food in and taking it out.

You need a sideboard or console table for food or dishes to be set on and served from. You also need one or more storage pieces, like a china chest, hutch, or breakfront, for linens, silverware, and china. A mixture of tall and low pieces of furniture is visually interesting. However, if space is limited, taller pieces, like armoires, Welsh cupboards, and wall shelves or cupboards hung above table height, provide ample storage without taking up much floor space. If your dining room is small, you can still include one large piece, perhaps the dining table, to enhance the room. However, if you prefer to capitalize on space, consider a glass-topped table, which consumes less visual space than a solid-topped one. Alternatively, choose a large table with removable leaves or an extension.

Dining Room Furniture Arranging and Tips

Deciding on dining room furniture and furniture placement is fairly easy because it is largely determined by the size and shape of your room. Here are helpful furnishing tips:

○ The focal point in a dining room is not usually the table. Create one or more focal points elsewhere— for example, wall art hung over a sideboard with two chairs flanking it, or a picture window, chandelier, or French doors.

○ If you have a combined living and dining room, make two focal points.

○ A table's shape affects the appearance of a room.

○ Round tables are great in square rooms.

○ Long tables make the best of long, narrow rooms.

○ Square tables work nicely in tiny dining rooms.

○ Round and square tables have no head or foot and tend to feel more casual.

○ Rectangular and oval tables are more formal.

○ Dining tables are usually in the center of the room.

SEATING

○ Be sure to have at least 3 feet (.9 meters) of pull-out space behind your dining chairs.

○ Use high-backed chairs in rooms with high ceilings.

○ Try open-backed chairs in small rooms.

○ To save space, pull a small love seat up to one side of a midsized table; use chairs on the other side.

○ If you are short on seating for a special gathering, pull card tables into the area and cover them with the same or similar cloths or even sheets; use a coffee table with floor pillows or TV tray tables for children.

You may want to sketch a floor plan of your dining room. It doesn't have to be drawn to scale, but you should note the length and width of the room. Indicate the approximate location of the electrical outlets, the location, height, and width of the windows, the swing of each door (left or right), and the width of each door (to make sure your furniture will fit through). This will enable you to determine the appropriate size for the furniture pieces. Bring your diagram with you if you need to shop for furniture or accessories.

FOR SMALL ROOMS

AVOID CHUNKY wooden tables.

TRY A DROP-LEAF table, a table with removable leaves, an expandable table, a fliptop table, or a narrow harvest table.

MAKE THE MOST of floor space by centering the table in front of a window; add focal point window treatments.

STORAGE AND SERVING

IN A SMALL ROOM, consider floor-to-ceiling shelves rather than a mid-height china cabinet to maximize available floor space and increase storage.

ATTACH A GRANITE or marble top to a simple side table for a great sideboard.

DRAPE FABRIC OVER a parson's table for an instant, inexpensive server with storage.

Dining Room Accessorizing Tips

○ Add 4 feet (1.2 meters) to the width and length of your dining room table to determine the minimum size of a rug for the room.

○ Use table settings to generate atmosphere in the eating area. Keep a variety of table coverings to suit your mood: a cloth or runner, quilts, a flatweave rug, table linens, and even a dining table slipcover made from fabric custom-tailored to fit your table.

○ Create seasonal table decorations and centerpieces. In autumn, use tiny Jack Be Little pumpkins, pepper berries, bayberries, nuts, apples, pomegranates, oranges, pinecones, fresh cranberries, and lemons studded with cloves. In summer, use seashells.

○ Place settings should be 20 to 24 inches (51 to 66 cm) wide.

○ Place a centerpiece at one end of the table so as not to obstruct the view of your guests during the meal. Alternatively, create a low centerpiece, perhaps using shiny fruits and vegetables, or place a mini bouquet in a tiny cordial glass at each place setting and omit the centerpiece.

○ Consider using a folding screen to reconfigure your room, hide the kitchen from the dining area, provide a temporary wall, or make a space to store things behind.

○ Hang a chandelier or pendant lamp so that the bottom is about 30 inches (76 cm) above the table. When the ceiling is higher than 8 feet (2.4 meters), balance the light by raising it 3 inches (8 cm) per additional foot. A hanging light's diameter should be at least 12 inches (30 cm) less than the length of the table.

○ Decorate your chandelier with silk or dried flowers, ribbons, or faux fruits.

○ Be sure to install a dimmer switch, which is essential to alter the atmosphere.

○ Make small dining rooms seem more intimate and warm with a rich or bold paint color. Green invites lingering and a sense of calm. Red stimulates appetite and conversation.

○ Increase visual space with accessories, such as a large mirror.

○ Use beautiful illustrations from old books on food-related topics, or your favorite restaurant menus, to make great wall art for your dining room. Frame them in similar or matching frames.

home offices

THE HOME OFFICE'S FUNCTION AND STYLE

The functionality of your home office is the most important aspect to consider when determining how to set it up; aesthetics comes next.

What has to be accomplished in your home office? Is it strictly for business? If you work at home full time, you probably want to locate your home office in a separate room. This could be your den, a spare bedroom, even a portion of the basement. You need grounded electrical outlets for a computer and a fax machine, and enough phone lines. You need plenty of work surfaces and storage. If clients visit your office, a room that has its own door to the outside is best suited to a professional image.

If you work part time or need a workplace for home-related duties such as bookkeeping and correspondence, you can use almost any room in the home that offers enough space for a desk or table, a computer, and storage. Will you be watching TV, reading, sleeping, or dressing in your home office? Find the best way to accommodate these activities.

Do you want your home office to have an air of formality and grace or an urban sophistication? Do you prefer a laid-back, cozy, casual space? Do you want to integrate your home office with an already decorated room?

[Robert Benchley] and I had an office so tiny that an inch smaller and it would have been adultery.

—DOROTHY PARKER

Soothing, simple, organized

WALLS
Glidden Aqua Tint #90GG 74/108

TRIM
Glidden Pure White

CABINETS
Glidden Aqua Chintz

ACCENT
Green, Cobalt Blue

ACCESSORY IDEAS
- Galvanized metal desk accessories
- Colored picture frames
- Wire file holders
- Painted bookshelves

island retreat

Work can be rewarding in more ways than one if you do it in this home office. Re-create the mood experienced on vacation—the enjoyment of cool summer breezes, aquamarine water, bright light, and silky air. Use the colors of sea glass to create a clean, cool, lustrous, and heavenly palette. Studies have proven that blue is the most soothing color, which is why the Navy chose the color blue for the inside of submarines. Blue also encourages meditative thinking and contemplation, and is, therefore, an appropriate choice for a home office. This simple color scheme is starkly beautiful and a pleasure to work in.

Custom design a workspace for yourself with furniture that is streamlined and simple, maintaining an understated and uncluttered look. Consider built-in, modular units. Add a large white Formica or wood table to use as a desk. Your chair can be a contrasting color, such as periwinkle blue. Repeat the color on your accessory pieces (waste basket, storage boxes, vases, lamps). Chrome or polished nickel brings some shimmer and interest to the room. Incorporate it in your lamps, table legs, chairs, and hardware. For extra storage, buy filing cabinets on casters. Window treatments are kept simple with the use of white roller shades. Be sure to get cord organizers to keep bundles of cables out of sight.

For a sensible and beautiful home office that is at once practical and serene, consider the colors of Island Retreat and begin to relax into your work. The power of color as it is used in this room is undeniable. It can truly enrich our lives.

Beauty seen is never lost.
God's colors are all fast.

—JOHN GREENLEAF WHITTIER

retro chic

The trend in decorating today, as in every aspect of life, is about simplifying. Life has gotten so complicated that even scheduling a casual dinner with friends is often a major production. Let the walls help do the decorating for you. In this home office, deep coral red was chosen to both stimulate and inspire. Vibrant, rich cobalt blue is meant to calm and sooth. The red wall and blue shutters stand out against the adjacent walls' softer pink hue. These are the perfect colors for a hardworking but creative environment.

Make a simple, but stylish retro decorating statement using stark, modern, functional furniture with a stripped-down aesthetic and an edge of playfulness. This type of furniture looks engineered rather than designed. It should be streamlined—molded plastic or metallic chairs; spindly tables with aluminum, stainless steel, or black metal legs; and lamps, also with metal bases and clean, sleek lines. Laminate finishes, such as Formica, and vinyl-covered or wood-topped furniture is widely produced today. Even industrial furniture can create a chic and sleek environment. Or, perhaps you prefer a modular furniture system with various components to suit your needs.

In terms of accessorizing, display less. Most of your objects should be stored away. Incorporate interesting lamps and a few favorite prints or photographs on the walls.

Choosing to decorate in a retro style requires a commitment to minimalist accessorizing and to keeping the area smooth and uncluttered.

Less is more.

—LUDWIG MIES VAN DER ROHE

Streamlined, playful, simple

WALLS
California Paints Coral Flower #7385

TRIM
California Paints Floral White

ACCENTS
Black, Blue, Pink

ACCESSORY IDEAS
- Streamlined lamps with metal bases
- Stainless or chrome picture frames, bowls
- Contemporary file boxes

Colorful, playful, casual, sophisticated

WALLS
Benjamin Moore Spring Purple
#2070-40

TRIM
Benjamin Moore Atrium White

ACCENTS
Red, Yellow, Blue

ACCESSORY IDEAS
- Brightly colored fabrics and accessories
- Large posters in bright graphics
- A favorite collection

cosmopolitan

Rooms that function as libraries or studies and hold loads of books provide the perfect spot for your home office. A large wooden desk in almost any style, along with a comfortable and interesting chair, like this modern model, bring a sense of playfulness to this restful room. Fabulous, brilliant crayon-colored brights fill the room with sparkle. Make the environment an amusing one filled with comfort, fun and vintage surprises, like this little coffee table.

Traditionally framed family photos blend perfectly with chic Manhattan roller window shades. Do combine unusual hand-crafted items along with colorful vinyl chairs, a bright solid or printed couch, upholstered chairs in bold colors, and multicolored pillows. Furnishings should share a unifying mood, playful and casual. Hang brightly colored artwork.

Are you tired of that dark wooden bureau in your bedroom? It would make ideal storage for computer paper and desk supplies in this office.

Simple things become beautiful and attractive
by an art inspiration. Interiors retain their old
forms substantially, but they put on new faces
when touched by the real artist.

—PALLISER'S AMERICAN ARCHITECTURE

Trick-or-Treat

An unused corner comes alive with a bright blue desk, a useful blue bracket shelf—and, just for fun, the addition of orange, blue's complement, in the form of a pumpkin.

The mood is laid-back and homey, with cool colors dominating and warm colors as accents. Sisal carpeting and simple, unpainted and painted furniture create textural and visual interest.

Accessorize shelves and surfaces with cheerful objects and hang photos of family pets, children, or even a finished jigsaw puzzle. Paint storage containers—boxes and baskets—in shades of blue.

Above all, this room functions efficiently and is comfortable, warm, and domestic in spirit. Although the walls are pale green, it is the color scheme of blue and orange, along with simplicity of design, that gives the room its impact and weaves the elements together, right down to the orange tags on the file drawers.

Life is not easy. I paint the memory of happiness.

—ANVAR SAIFOUTDINOV

Homey, simple, fun

WALLS
Glidden Pale Wintergreen #24GY 85/110

TRIM
Glidden Antique White

ACCENTS
Blue, Orange

ACCESSORY IDEAS
- Family prints or photos
- Rugs or carpet in neutral honey and caramel tones
- Orange accessories
- Chrome lamps
- Metal file box

Low-key, polished

WALLS
Glidden Surrey Beige #30YY 36/185

TRIM
Glidden Pure White

ACCENT
Turquoise

ACCESSORY IDEAS
- Antique or oversized clock
- Oak and painted chairs
- Plants
- Industrial lamps
- Stacking baskets

earthy office

Taupe is a classic shade associated with the earthlike qualities of brown, such as comfort, normalcy, and security. It is very easy to live and work with, creating a sophisticated mood and understated appearance. And, it is a favorite neutral to combine with other colors. In an office, taupe seems most at home. This earthy office is low-key, laid-back, and yet professional and polished in style.

White trim, a white desktop, and drawers bring in a suggestion of sunshine, brightening the heaviness of the atmosphere. For a striking statement that still has the comfort factor, use a black desk as an accent. Make the room upbeat with a surprising splash of color, such as the turquoise blue on this painted chair. This office has a somewhat masculine feel, incorporating an oak library swivel chair, industrial aluminum swing lamps, and heavy-duty aluminum trash bucket. But this taupe paint color has no gender. A quick switch of accessories makes the room suitable for anyone. Bring in a floral-hooked rug to place in front of the desk. Use floral seat cushions and fabric window treatments. Have plants near you. Little touches mean everything as you construct your workspace. Add baskets in various shapes and sizes. An oversized wall clock is nice, but an antique desk clock is lovely too. Shelves can serve as display areas for books, or as a storage area for supplies and equipment.

The tree that moves some to tears of joy is in the eyes of others only a green thing that stands in the way. Some see nature all ridicule and deformity... and some scarce see it at all. But to the eyes of the man of imagination, nature is imagination itself.

—WILLIAM BLAKE

home office furniture

CORE FURNITURE

- writing desk or table and chair
- computer table or unit
- storage units (file cabinets, bookcases)

The goal here is to arrange the furniture efficiently so all of the essentials of your home office are handy. You may decide to heighten the attention to design by identifying a focal point, such as an ornately carved desk, and arranging the furniture around it, or you may prefer to place your furniture in an L or U configuration for easy access.

Do you have a surface large enough for both writing and computer work? It is a good idea, if not essential, to have both. Depending on your style sensibility, you can use anything from an old kitchen table to an antique table or desk.

How much seating do you need? You want a comfortable chair for yourself and perhaps additional seating in the room—a reclining chair, an upholstered chair, or a love seat.

Storage is critical in the home office. Modular storage pieces come with many options such as shelves, doors, and drawers. They come in many styles as well, from casual laminates to sleek, chic, burnished aluminum. Consider freestanding furniture from other rooms in your home for storage, such as armoires, cupboards, hutches, sideboards—even a painted chest of drawers. You may also need bookshelves. Use freestanding units or have them built in. File cabinets can be attractive as well as functional if you choose, for example, a vintage antique oak cabinet. New file cabinets are available in a wide variety of finishes, including wood, metal, and laminate.

Your storage pieces can be versatile. Consider old trunks and lidded benches that can double as tables or seats, and stacked boxes, baskets, and bowls.

Make your work experience as pleasant as possible with a highly functional, efficient, and aesthetically meaningful home office.

Home Office Furniture Arranging and Tips

- Use an old drop-leaf table to extend your work space.

- Consider placing your desk at an angle to provide a more generous work area and to visually widen the room.

- Convert ordinary chests to office-ware with hanging files and special drawer inserts.

- Consider closet organizer systems to help with storage.

- Add a bistro table and chairs in a tiny spot for writing and for a coffee or tea break.

- House your fax machine and printer in a beautiful, decorative, open metal display cabinet.

For reference: Standard desks are 30 inches (76 cm) high. File cabinets come with 15 by 29-inch (38 by 74 cm) letter-size drawers; legal-size drawers are 3 inches (8 cm) wider. Computer and typewriter stands are usually 26 inches (66 cm) high.

Carefully consider the location of electrical outlets and phone lines when deciding where to place your furniture. Measure the size of your doorways to be sure they will accommodate the passage of your furniture. Do you have a wonderful treasured desk you want to feature in the room? If so, position the desk in the room first. Sketch a floor plan or try to visualize the furniture in the room before placing it.

Home Office Accessorizing Tips

- For a touch of elegance and to visually expand the space, hang an antique mirror over the desk.

- Consider floating the desk away from the wall.

- Warm the space with Oriental and other rugs.

- Give your old chair(s) a lift with new fabric seat cushions.

- Add a view by hanging a mirrored window panel on the wall for a faux window effect.

- Use old fire andirons as bookends.

- Install shutters and miniblinds, which are practical window coverings for the home office. Soften the look with fabric curtains.

- Supplement desk lamps with decorative accent lights.

- Consider recessed or track lighting for your general lighting.

- Consider lighting the inside of tall storage units.

- To direct the eye away from the clutter of office supplies, use a strong paint color on the walls and restrict the use of patterned fabrics.

- Conceal a file cabinet with a fabric table skirt. Set a ¼-inch (.5 cm)-thick piece of plywood cut into a circle on the cabinet and drape it with fabric to the floor.

bedrooms

THE BEDROOM'S FUNCTION AND STYLE

The bedroom should, first and foremost, provide a sense of comfort. This is where you escape the day's chaos and rejuvenate. During the evening hours, or in the morning, when daylight breaks, this room may be a gathering place for your family. But at night, the roles you have played all day can be put to rest, and you can pamper yourself. Create a sense of luxury and convenience. You may crave a dreamy retreat complete with a large four-poster or canopy bed loaded with downy pillows and a featherbed. Maybe your cat has a cozy sleeping spot here. Perhaps you prefer a tailored, modern bed in a minimal, sparsely decorated setting where fabric and form are most important. For a die-hard music lover, a great sound system may be a real luxury in the bedroom. Assess what you need to feel truly comfortable. The bedroom is your place to shed the cares of the day, unwind, watch movies, read, and sleep.

Keep in mind the function of your bedroom as you decorate it. Good storage is second only to comfort. You want lots of space to stow your wearables and easy access to all of it. Determine how much storage you need. Is your bedroom for sleeping only or for other activities as well, like watching TV? Do you need a desk or table? How much natural light is there? Do you need to block out morning light or street noise? Do you need thick carpet and fabrics to absorb sound? Regardless of your style preferences, you want easy access to the telephone, TV remote, alarm clock, and books.

The ideal bedroom is as inviting as a room at your favorite resort or inn—comfortable, efficient, and beautiful.

No matter how big or soft or warm your bed is, you still have to get out of it.

—GRACE SLICK

Whimsical, tranquil

WALLS
Benjamin Moore Mystical Grape
#2071-30

TRIM
Benjamin Moore Brilliant White

ACCENTS
Magenta

ACCESSORY IDEAS
- Berry-colored pillows
- Antique quilts
- Painted furniture pieces
- Whimsical rugs
- Antique glass lamps

eternal blue

Blue is a favorite choice for bedrooms because of its relaxing feel. If your bedroom is the place you like to unwind, consider this cobalt blue with strong violet undertones. As Swiss psychologist Dr. Max Luscher stated in his book, *Four Color Person* (Pocket Books, Simon and Schuster, 1979): "Just sit down in front of a dark blue color and see what kind of mood it produces in you. You will feel a motionless calm, a relaxed satisfaction, an endless sense of harmony and contentment will come over you."

Wouldn't you love to wake up in this bedroom? Bring a sense of peace and tranquility to your spirit and paint the bedroom violet blue. Any style home can handle strong color in a bedroom. Even an old house like this one need not be painted with traditional colors. Bring the room to life with the bright, fruity colors of summertime. These walls make a luscious backdrop for colorful coral and berry red bed pillows. A cheerful antique quilt adds a strong design element, as does the whimsical print rug. The colors in this rug echo those of the main wall color and the accent colors on the bedding. A pale green painted table introduces yet another color surprise. This green is subtly repeated in a delicate vine pattern on the pillowcase. Old clear or colored glass lamp bases are a nice accent with white or multicolored lampshades. Core furniture such as the bed and dresser can be old or new pieces, in wood tones ranging anywhere from light to dark. The room holds an eclectic mix.

Relax, refresh, and replenish both your body and soul with this Eternal Blue bedroom.

A blue surface seems to return from us...but as we readily follow an agreeable object that flies from us, so we love to contemplate blue, not because it advances to us, but because it draws us after it.

—GOETHE

penthouse view

Whether you live in a high-rise apartment or not, you can combine high design with comfort to achieve the penthouse look. The quickest route to success is to use black and white furnishings with accent colors only. Display craft objects from fine galleries alongside a favorite framed photograph or map on an easel. Place collectibles such as ceramic vases and bowls on shelves and family photos on a contemporary end table. Hang framed, enlarged black-and-white photographs. Be selective.

Float your furniture groupings away from the walls, if you have a large enough room. Modular furniture units are suitable. Include a round breakfast table covered in cloth for lazy weekend mornings. Pile books on contemporary art and world architecture on bookshelves. Eliminate window treatments, or keep windows sparse; simple side panels, pleated fabric, or wooden shades are plenty.

Arrange all your furniture proportionate in size, allowing the eyes to flow straight to the focal point in the room—a window, in this case. The focal point might also be a fireplace or wall-hung artwork. Use this sophisticated blue-green paint color for the walls.

You don't have to have a view of Central Park or a bluestone patio to give your home penthouse appeal.

Any time you see a turtle atop a fence post, you know it had some help.

—ALEX HALEY

Sophisticated, modern

WALLS
Benjamin Moore Mountain Laurel #AC-20

TRIM
Benjamin Moore Atrium White

ACCENTS
Gold, Black, White

ACCESSORY IDEAS
- Books on contemporary art and world architecture
- Framed black-and-white photographs
- Wooden window shades and simple side panels
- Contemporary crafts
- Simple striped throw pillows

Soft, serene, luxurious

WALLS
Benjamin Moore Hibiscus #2027-50

TRIM
Benjamin Moore Atrium White

ACCENTS
Yellow, Coral

ACCESSORY IDEAS
- Floral paintings or prints
- Floral bed linens
- Piles of pillows in beautiful fabrics
- Framed family photos
- Vintage hats
- Oval mirror with satin ribbon hanger

dahlias and peonies

More and more, people are becoming do-it-yourselfers when it comes to gardening. The process is one of fascinating discovery. As you weed and rearrange plantings, you inevitably learn more and more about them. If you happen upon a large, unfamiliar root or bulb while digging around the yard, it might actually be worth saving. For example, if you see a turniplike root, transplant it. In a couple of years, you might just have a fantastic, enormous peony plant covered with fragrant, plump blush-pink blossoms. According to the ancient Greeks, peonies moan when they are picked, and anyone within earshot of this sound will die of it. They must have had their reasons for keeping the blossoms attached to the plant.

This room, featuring framed dahlia prints and peony pillows, is intended to be your private sanctuary—restful and quiet. Before you do anything else, choose and position the bed, which is the focal point in this room. Use a wooden bed painted white, as this one is, or consider a canopy bed, brass bed, four-poster, or sleigh bed. Cast iron bed frames painted white are beautiful, or use a daybed in a tight space. Make your bed the magnificent feature. Dress it in matelassé or Battenberg lace, with pastel linens in complementary florals and solids. Luxuriate in the softest Egyptian cotton sheets. This is an ideal setting for your jewelry chest, lingerie chest, and armoire. A painted white floor or deep pile carpet adds to the soft look. Drape side tables with a fabric skirt and an organza or lace overlay. Suspend floral or other botanical prints or an oval mirror from lovely velvet or satin ribbons with bows. You might also hang a collection of vintage hats. Scatter beautifully framed photos of your family about the room. Use crystal candy dishes to hold rings. Display pretty crystal sculptures. Grace the surface of a bureau or table with a vintage brush and comb set. Incorporate the shy pink of the peony in the color scheme.

The universe is made of stories, not atoms.

—MURIEL RUKEYSER

Contemporary country, serene

scandinavian minimal

Anyone new to decorating can ensure perfection with this recipe. It is restful yet dramatic in its own simple way. Contemporary-style furniture is perfect for achieving a minimalist effect. This room may have pine, oak, or wicker furniture. The look is monochromatic and neutral, with clean, sleek lines. Lamps are simple and small. Keep the bed streamlined and understated; choose white bedding and window treatments. Remove the ruffles and layers. Add a box-pleat bed skirt. Pull off the throw pillows and instead arrange a maximum of four full-sized pillows. Stick to solid linens or small, subtle, pale prints on sheets. Position special art objects under a skylight or beside a window. For added color, hang a striking piece of contemporary art or framed poster. Complement this sophisticated and serene room with interesting items that surprise the eye, like a piece of sculpture, the bare branch of a large tree, or a cluster of pussy willows in a floor vase or umbrella stand in a corner. Store your stuff behind closed doors or in baskets.

You can readily achieve professional-looking results with this Scandinavian-style bedroom.

WALLS
Benjamin Moore Paper White
#OC-55

TRIM
Benjamin Moore Atrium White

ACCENTS
Wood Tones, Pale Brown, Red

ACCESSORY IDEAS
- Single piece of sculpture
- Large framed contemporary art print
- Willow branches
- Simple tall vase

Whatever path of action you find that brings good and happiness to all, follow this way like the moon in the path of stars.

—ANONYMOUS

Refined, country

WALLS
California Paints Peruvian Violet
#7013

TRIM
California Paints Floral White

ACCENTS
Blue, Pink, Blue/green

ACCESSORY IDEAS
◦ Oval framed silhouettes
◦ Colored glass bottles
◦ Elegant solid curtains with
  decorative detailing
◦ White bedspread with decorative
  detailing

wedgwood colors

Most of us are familiar with the classic, stunning stoneware called Wedgwood, which epitomizes a refined, classic soft style of decorating. All Wedgwood colors are matched to antique cameos. They always have a dusty matte finish, and this room takes on a similar quality—like a summer breeze, a soft mist. Accent colors are muted, like the cream color of pale moon lilies or dusty rose. Mix with white or burnished gold accessories.

This room is calming and serene. A wicker chair adorned with an antique quilt throw adds texture. Use a neutral rug. Include a lovely, elegant bedside table. For a warmer environment, also include a rich wooden dresser.

Add luxurious curtain panels with decorative detailing. Accessorize with colored glass bottles and candles in colors that look like cameos or alabaster. Hang small oval frames containing family silhouettes or pressed herbs.

O'er her warm cheek and
rising bosom move
The bloom of young desire
and purple light of love.

—ANONYMOUS

matisse's colors

Matisse, probably more than any other painter, is known for his use of color. The balanced color in his works have proven timeless in interior decorating. The fresh, vivid, whimsical, uplifting combinations once thought arbitrary and shocking have become widely accepted for use in homes and are alive and refreshing today. We feel comfortable surrounded by the mood Matisse created.

Use this scheme in a teenager's bedroom. Start with a background that will set off the furnishings: walls in white or a strong color, like green. Place a large piece of furniture (it need not be the bed), perhaps in a bold color or fabric, against this. If you are adventuresome, try to hand-stencil the walls with moons, stars, dancing figures, fruit, leaves, or oversized blossoms. Cover the bed with brightly colored and patterned pillows that make the most of contrasting colors and strong graphics, like stars. Incorporate a homemade screen to make a dressing area or to disguise clutter. Enhance comfort and coziness with deep chairs, a side table with reading lamps and houseplants. Combine primary colors on rugs with surprise print fabrics, like tartan plaid. A playful, fresh, homey mood is the goal. Load colorful ceramic vases with flowers or greens, like silver-dollar eucalyptus. Set out perfume bottles and boxes of jewelry or hang jewelry, scarves, and hats from the back of a chair, wall pegs, or a hat rack. Pictures need not be framed. Bring a fun-loving spirit into the bedroom.

My canvases that are simply drawn...are more profoundly moving...like the tears of a child in its cradle.

—HENRI MATISSE

Playful, vivid, casual

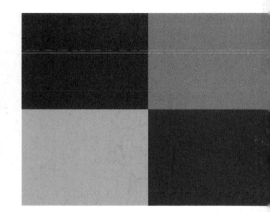

WALLS
Glidden Arbor Green #30GY 30/267

TRIM
Glidden White High Hidding

ACCENTS
Red, Gold, Violet, Navy Blue

ACCESSORY IDEAS
° Matisse prints
° Bright solid fabrics, accent only with printed fabrics
° Irregular and unconventional furniture
° Colorful ceramic vases
° Whimsical motif stenciled on wall or painted on furniture
° Colorful scarves and jewelry hung on a chair, coat, or hat rack

Light, open, airy, neutral

WALLS
Benjamin Moore Wickham Gray
HC-171

TRIM
Benjamin Moore White Dove

ACCENTS
Black, Green

ACCESSORY IDEAS
- Tall table and floor lamps with pale colored shades
- Pale, pickled mirror frame(s)
- Wrought iron or light wood curtain rods
- Sisal rugs
- Plants
- Textured, tone-on-tone, neutral fabrics

coastal dreams

The first step to creating a coastal-style bedroom is to open the windows to let the outdoors in. Replace heavy draperies with minimal window treatments, like gauzy sheers or simple shades. Notice the natural light and feel as though you are bringing your garden indoors.

This bedroom style is simple, easy, minimal, and somewhat elegant. The neutral, putty-colored tones of sand and stone as well as the greens and blues of the sea and sky make up the color scheme. The atmosphere is light and airy. Emphasize texture rather than color on fabrics and furniture. Fabrics, including bedding, are subtle, muted; excellent choices are silk, chenille, soft tapestry, and white canvas. Use these neutral textures and tones throughout the room. Layer fabrics on the bed, making the total effect downy, soft, casual, but elegant with down comforters. The subtle fabric patterns are easy to mix because they are essentially interchangeable. You are working with texture, not color.

Furniture is usually pale wood, often pickled (a washy, bleached white paint) with a European, particularly Spanish-style, design. Alternatively, introduce cream-colored French night tables. Explore the generous use of wrought iron and pale colored stone, especially travertine marble. In this style, furniture is often overscaled; even lamps are taller. Lamp shades are usually white or off-white. Sisal rugs and area rugs placed over sisal are appropriate to the style.

The entire environment is light, with a few black accents found in iron on table bases and lamps. Plants are welcome in this room, and a palm tree is perfect. You don't need to live in a Spanish style or a California ranch house to enjoy a coastal-style home.

God's first creature, which was light.

—FRANCIS BACON

bedroom furniture

CORE FURNITURE

- bed
- storage chest(s) (drawers, armoire, vanity, modular units)
- night tables

Due to its size, the bed is the focal point of most bedrooms. Position your bed in the room first. Traffic should be able to flow around it easily. You need at least 2 feet (.6 meters) on each side of the bed to approach it comfortably. If you already have a wonderful bed, great! If not, try one of these ideas:

- Instant canopy: Drape a mosquito-netting veil over the bed from a hook or wooden ring attached to the ceiling.
- Enclosed bed: Hang four rods the length and width of the bed from the ceiling, then suspend drapes from them. Pocket drapes and tab curtains work well.
- Hang ceiling-to-floor pocket drapes from a pole on the full length of the wall behind the bed, or some portion of it.
- Buy an old wooden four-poster or otherwise interesting old bed in sound condition and revive it with paint. Try a creamy white or black.
- Exploit an interesting headboard and footboard or a wall treatment behind the bed to increase its value as a focal point.

CONSIDER THESE:

- Hang an old door sideways on the wall above the bed or use another architectural piece, like picket fencing, garden latticework, or an iron gate instead of a headboard.
- Install a simple shelf spanning the width of the bed. Use attractive brackets to hang it. Then place books and other accessories on it.
- Use pegs to hang a panel of fabric from the ceiling to the floor behind the bed.
- Hang a large painting or three smaller paintings over the bed as a focal point.
- Paint a design onto a piece of wood sized to fit behind your bed. Affix it to the wall as a headboard.

Bedside tables should be at least as high as the top of your mattress. Use anything from conventional nightstands to a pile of old stacked suitcases as a side table. If your bedroom is small, consider using your bureau as a nightstand. Let the style of your bedroom (or the recipe you select) assist you in choosing side tables. Be sure the surface has enough room for lighting, an alarm clock, the phone, and tissues.

Choose a chest or two of drawers, an armoire or cupboard, a dress-mirror combination, or modular storage for clothing. Include an armchair and ottoman, a love seat, or a chaise lounge in the bedroom if you have the space. Use it for reading or to toss your pillows and clothing onto. Other furniture you may want to include: a vanity, jewelry chest, chair with an ottoman, a bench at the end of the bed, a desk or writing table, and a TV stand or unit. Even one piece of large-scale furniture makes a small bedroom seem larger. Try a four-poster bed without fabric bed hangings (which block the view) or an armoire.

Break the rules in a guest bedroom. Instead of a standard bed, use a sofa bed, daybed, futon, or flip-open sofa. These can be transformed with the addition of a featherbed over the mattress and good bed pillows. Because this room won't be used every day, you don't need to be as concerned about practicality, so you could use a footstool as a bedside table, for instance, and a clamp-on lamp for nighttime reading.

Bedroom Furniture Arranging and Tips

- Allow 3 feet (.9 meters) or more in front of your closet for dressing.

- Allow 36 to 40 inches (91 to 102 cm) in front of chests and dressers to pull the drawers out.

- Allow 2 feet (.6 meters) or more around the bed.

IF THE ROOM IS SMALL:

- Use a few large pieces of furniture rather than a lot of small pieces. This reduces clutter.

- Place furniture parallel or perpendicular to the wall (furniture placed on a diagonal may take up too much floor space).

- Use tall rather than wide or short storage pieces.

- Choose furniture with a light finish, as dark finishes take up more visual space.

- Leave ample open space around large objects such as armoires and dressers.

Start with the most important piece of furniture: the bed. Decide where to put it first. Then sketch or visualize a floor plan for the additional furniture. Be aware of the location of the electrical outlets and windows.

Bedroom Accessorizing Tips

◦ Choose a rug no larger than 3 feet (.9 meters) narrower and 3 feet (.9 meters) shorter than the room itself.

◦ Consider nightstands with drawers or doors to camouflage books, magazines, tissues, pens, paper, crossword puzzles.

◦ Select window treatments capable of blocking morning light.

◦ Try hanging a mirror directly across from a window to create the impression of more light and more windows.

◦ Hang scarves, jewelry, and belts from Shaker-style pegs or wall hooks.

◦ Group perfume bottles and paraphernalia on a tray or within a box to unify the collection.

◦ Take advantage of closet organizers that feature racks, shelves, drawers, cubbies.

◦ For a pleasant change, consider varying bed linens with the seasons. Choose from the nicest cottons and flannels.

◦ Add warmth and color with a potted flowering plant.

◦ Try this great bed-pillow combination: two 26-inch (56 cm)-square European pillows with shams against the headboard, two standard or king-size pillows in front of them, and two neck rolls or one breakfast pillow in front of them all.

◦ In smaller rooms, use a scrolled metal headboard, which consumes less visual space than a carved wooden headboard of the same size.

◦ When guests arrive to stay in your guest bedroom, welcome them with fresh flowers, mints on the pillow, tourist information, several best-selling books, magazines, maps, wrapped snacks, a radio, and a clock.

Bedroom Lighting Tips

◦ Choose lamps and lightbulbs with three-way switches.

◦ Use a pair of lamps for formal balance.

◦ To save tabletop space, choose swing-arm lamps or install sconces above night tables.

◦ Install recessed lights with a dimmer for good but unobtrusive general lighting.

◦ In a particularly fancy bedroom, hang a chandelier with a dimmer over the bed.

◦ Add architectural interest with halogen track lights.

For reference, bedroom lamps are usually 22 to 28 inches (56 to 71 cm) tall.

children's bedrooms

THE CHILD'S BEDROOM FUNCTION AND STYLE

In a child's room, safety takes precedence over aesthetics. Keep this in mind during the decorating process. A child's room also must be adaptable, because it will probably be redone or adjusted several times.

First, the room will be set up for your baby/toddler. The first room redo will probably be during your child's early school years and the second during his or her teenage years. You can start decorating from scratch for each stage in your child's life, choose furnishings that will grow with your child through the years, or do a bit of both. Your decorating will have greater longevity if you emphasize sturdiness and function of furniture before style.

Determine if your child's room will be used for sleeping only, or for both sleep and play. Will the room be shared by more than one child. Maybe you want a combination bedroom/playroom. Will your child use his or her room for homework? Will he or she draw or do arts and crafts projects and other activities there? How will the room be used now, and how do you anticipate it being used in the future? Factor this into your furniture choices.

Most children's rooms are casual in style. However, a formal style works in children's rooms, too. Choose matching furniture or classic styles, like antiques. Include a wonderful bed. Choose window treatments and other fabrics as you would for a formal adult bedroom, such as full length drapes, but with decidedly child-appropriate prints. Try to keep your child's needs in mind and maintain a sense of fun, wonder, and whimsy.

To get more decorating mileage out of the room, you might want to avoid themes (bunnies, ballerinas) on the walls and furniture, reserving them instead for more easily replaced accessories such as bedsheets and artwork. Interesting paint colors and classic patterned fabrics, such as stripes, florals, and checks, can be used throughout the room at any of the three decorating stages without requiring change.

Perhaps you will want a different decorating look for all three stages of your child's development and want the pleasure of decorating the room each time. It's all up to you and your children.

Nothing can be truer than fairy wisdom. It is as true as sunbeams.

—DOUGLAS TERROLD

Whimsical, busy, stimulating

WALLS
Glidden Pink Lemonade 90RR 69/101

TRIM
Glidden White High Hidding

ACCENTS
Green, Red

ACCESSORY IDEAS
- Hand-painted wall motifs
- Print wall-to-wall carpet
- Colorful pillows
- Colorful painted buckets and boxes
  for storage

nui's house

On workdays, some lucky children go to Nui's house after school. It's more than a day care center; the place is full of magic. In summertime, kids can go blueberry picking, hammock swinging, apple tree climbing, and skinny-dipping in wading pools, then eat Concord grapes fresh off the vine.

In autumn, they roll apples under the fences to the horses and ponies, jump into piles of leaves, hang upside down from the monkey bars in the tree house, and get spooked by scads of scary electronic witches and goblins displayed in the house.

In winter, they go downstairs to the playroom and slide down the old, wide, metal slide to belly-first landings in piles of pillows. Electronic Santas and hundreds of wooden rocking horse ornaments hang from the ceiling in the kitchen bay window. The kids ooh over a tree of angels and a big gingerbread house they get to eat after Christmas. Moms get fresh eggs from the hens at 75 cents per half-dozen.

In spring, hundreds of perennials bloom, and the kids feed the chickens fresh grass, dig in the huge sandbox, and roll down the plastic roller coaster.

Nui's house has aquariums full of fish having fish babies, jars filled with colorful candies, dogs barking, cats frolicking, and colorful flags and banners. This happy place is full of love and bursting with color. It's an eclectic mix combining comfort and whimsy. The best thing of all is when kids get to stay for sleepovers in Nui's wonderful bedrooms.

This room is a playful compilation of everything your child loves. It features plush toys, a window seat/toy box, a hand-painted teapot motif on walls, and a kid-sized table and chairs for "cooking" and art projects. For your room, consider unfinished furniture for a side table, desk, chair, bookshelf, and bureau. Paint each drawer a different color if you like. How about bunk beds? Add whimsical hooks and drawer pulls in the shape of your choice—perhaps leaves, bumblebees, or ladybugs. Make instant cubbies with tall, painted CD racks. You can buy paints at your local paint store that turn walls into chalkboards or magnetic surfaces. Incorporate mismatched linens. Hot-glue pompom, bead, or tassled trim to window shades. Mix colors and furnishings as you like, but stick to your color scheme to be sure color weaves the room together (see appendix B).

I remember, I remember,
The house where I was born,
The little window where the sun
Came peeping in at morn.

—THOMAS HOOD

Pink is a baby's cheek, a soft Southern breeze.
Gray is a shawl around the shoulders. Brown is
withered hands, warm friendly leaf mold, the
trunks of aged trees. Lilac is the loved, kissed
face. Yellow is the sun, the rich promise of life.

—HELEN KELLER

baby mine

There is nothing like the indescribable sweetness of a new baby. It can only be experienced by holding a baby close, feeling its softness, breathing in its gentle smell, and hearing its tiny coos. It is a precious miracle one can savor for what eventually seems only a moment before it is replaced with an altogether different experience as we get to know our toddlers.

A beautiful but bittersweet scene in the Disney movie *Dumbo* captures the special bond between mama and baby. Baby Dumbo is being cradled and rocked in his mama's trunk as she sings him a lullaby, "Baby Mine," from her cage. If you are pregnant and you intend to watch this scene, keep the tissue box handy, as you are sure to well up with tears.

Simplicity is perfect in a baby's room. Your baby needs the basics: a crib that meets current safety standards, a changing table high enough for you to keep from straining your back, storage for clothing and toys, and a rocker or glider chair, with or without an ottoman.

You will accumulate lots of paraphernalia once the baby arrives, so you don't want to load the room with too many cute knick-knacks right now. Try to stick to basics and a few lovely accessories, like interesting and stimulating toys. Babies do not use crib quilts or pillows—just a sheet, bumper, and perhaps a small fleece blanket. If you buy all the crib beddings, understand that they are for decoration. Put the quilt on the wall. Handcrafted and antique items are beautiful in a baby's room, but be sure they are well out of reach.

A mix of furnishings and accessories rather than an entirely matched set of furniture and color-coordinated accessories make for a more interesting space. For extra storage, white Formica closets you assemble yourself are nondescript but practical. This room is a good opportunity to use interesting color on the wall. The items you display will change as your baby grows older, so make the wall color important in your color scheme. Choose pretty baskets and boxes for storage, interesting, perhaps antique shelves, a hand-painted toy box, a wicker changing table, and wall art baby cannot reach or pull down. Incorporate different pieces held together with a color scheme (see appendix B) and the baby theme.

Simple, serene

WALLS
California Paints Moonless Morn
#8463M

TRIM
California Paints Floral White

ACCENTS
Red, Yellow

ACCESSORY IDEAS
◦ Wicker baskets and boxes
◦ Color-coordinated fabrics on crib bedding and upholstery
◦ Wall shelf for toys and stuffed animals
◦ Standing shelf unit for toys, slippers, books

Whimsical, lively

WALLS
Benjamin Moore Lavender Mist #2070
Benjamin Moore Etched Glass #2006

TRIM
Benjamin Moore Brilliant White

ACCENTS
Yellow, Pink

ACCESSORY IDEAS
- Stuffed animals
- Book baskets
- Globe or atlas
- Colorful storage containers
- Framed art projects

puppy dogs' tails

This recipe is designed for a little boy as both a bedroom and a playroom. Boys love to build and move, so the space is functional, sturdy, and open. There is plenty of room to be creative, learn, explore, and dream. Favorite motifs for boy's rooms run the gamut from trucks, trains, cars, sailing ships, steamboats, wild animals, and dinosaurs to Curious George, Peter Rabbit, and Pooh. If a theme is important to your child, incorporate it in the accessories, such as rugs, pillows, stuffed animals, or wallpaper borders. Once your child has outgrown the theme, it will be much easier, both physically and economically, to remove these related accents from the room than it would be to redecorate entirely.

Contrasting paint colors—purple and green—make the most of the playful collection of toys and accessories displayed throughout the room. Repeat these colors on fabric pillows and upholstery. Keep the room tidy, with lots of storage pieces such as cabinets to hide secret treasures in and shelves with bins for blocks, books, cherished items, and knick-knacks. Use small touches of bright color to connect the storage to the room's decor. A freestanding bed looks great, but a built-in bed with its own privacy curtain is a special retreat. Under-the-bed drawers provide additional storage. Let the room be fun for your child. Informal, comfortable, sturdy furniture is fine; it doesn't have to match.

Whimsical, colorful prints dominate. Vary your fabrics for bedding, window treatments, furniture, and accessories. Place a low pile rug down for color and comfort. Your child's individuality should be encouraged. Display objects that will be used and that are meaningful to your child. Enlarge a favorite vacation photo and make it into a throw pillow. Tuck photos and birthday invitations into mirror frames. Hang your child's framed artwork. Pile books into baskets.

You cannot decorate a room before you know its gender.

—JOAN KRON, *HOME-PSYCH* (1983)

children's bedroom furniture

CORE FURNITURE

BABY/TODDLER
- crib
- changing table
- rocker or glider chair
- chest(s) of drawers

EARLY SCHOOL YEARS
- bed(s)
- side table(s)
- chest(s) of drawers
- shelves

ADOLESCENT
- desk

Children's bedrooms are first decorated for a baby/toddler, with a crib and changing table/storage, a rocking chair or glider with an ottoman, and a chest of drawers. If space permits, include a daybed or twin-size bed. This convenience can remain when the crib is removed.

Safety takes precedence—so, for example, keep the area around the crib clear of accessories like artwork, shelves, or anything that can be pulled off the wall by the baby. Use hook-and-loop fabric, such as Velcro, or picture hangers to secure artwork and mirrors to the wall. Avoid excessive bedding and pillows in the crib unless you plan to take them out before the baby goes in.

You will need to redo or make adjustments to the room during the early school years and again in the teen years. Some furniture pertains to a specific stage of development—for example, the crib. During the early school years, many kids spend endless hours at a small square or round table with a chair, drawing and doing puzzles and other projects. You may want to include one in your child's bedroom. If the room serves as a play-room, you might include a slide or climbing cube.

A desk is something to consider once your child is a teenager, or perhaps even sooner. A sturdy chest of drawers will endure and can remain in the room throughout all three stages. Likewise, a bookshelf is flex-ible enough to be used for baby supplies and toys, then later for volumes of books.

Child's Bedroom Furniture Arranging and Tips

◦ In general, keep furniture against the walls, leaving the floor area open for play and free of furniture that can be bumped into.

◦ Ensure that traffic flows easily through the room. Keep doorways and windows free of clutter. Plan a fire exit.

◦ Use fabric to dress up a plain bed and transform it into a fancy or formal bed. Create a faux canopy by suspending fabric from the ceiling.

◦ Choose laminates, plastics, and painted surfaces for furniture finishes, as these are durable choices.

◦ Save space with bunk beds and under-the-bed drawers.

Child's Bedroom Accessorizing Tips

- Consider murals and decorative paint treatments.

- Try a special wall finish, such as blackboard paint (just like a real chalkboard, in a wide variety of colors; frame it with painted trim) or metallic paint (comes in colors, works just like a refrigerator does. You can put up artwork with magnets).

- Choose low pile carpet, woven rugs, and bare wood floors, which are most practical.

- Install low rods in closet that kids can reach.

- Install peg racks at children's height.

- Install open shelves on the wall for stacking bins and baskets, as nursery schools do. Toys are then easy to see and to reach.

- Suspend a plastic ceiling-to-floor chain with hooks for stuffed animals, socks, or shoes.

bathrooms

THE BATHROOM'S FUNCTION AND STYLE

When it comes to relaxation, most women put taking a bath at the top of their list. Where else in the house can you go and really be left alone? We all want our bathroom to be clean, private, practical, and, perhaps, luxurious.

In decorating the bathroom, ask yourself, "Am I in and out, or do I linger?" Do you apply your makeup and fix your hair in the bathroom? Do you spend time soaking in the tub? The more time you spend in the bathroom, the more you may want to include luxury and spa-type amenities.

We all need a bathing area and a grooming/makeup area. We need surfaces to rest items on. We need storage and containers for toiletries and towels—anything from under-vanity storage to straw baskets to small chests and shelves. Whether you have a high-tech spa-style bath or a modest tub/shower combo, the bottom line on function is to get yourself clean and relaxed, see a well-lit reflection in the mirror, enjoy ample storage, and perhaps exploit a chair, table, or stool for resting and tossing clothing or towels onto.

If you are remodeling a bathroom, the style choices for tile, fixtures, hardware, cabinetry, tub, and shower can be overwhelming. Narrow your choices by reading the bathroom recipes here and by studying photos of baths in home magazines.

My whole idea of life is that French song "La Vie en Rose"—everything gentle.

—DOLLY HOFFMAN

Adventurous, nautical

WALLS
Benjamin Moore Citron #2024-30,
Benjamin Moore Orange Sky #2018-10

ACCENT
White

ACCESSORY IDEAS
◦ Framed maps
◦ Wooden towel and magazine racks
◦ Striped cotton rugs
◦ Colorful bottles
◦ Shells and driftwood

caribbean cruise

A Caribbean cruise inspired this bathroom. Vivid, radiant orange and yellow walls are accented with round mirrors that mimic portholes. You can almost imagine peering out to the waves below. Blue and white tiles are suggestive of the water and are quintessentially nautical colors. A natural wood tub surround and shelf bring the outdoors in. Visits to this bath immediately conjure up images of a tropical vacation where relaxation is paramount.

Everything about orange is luminous, hot, cheerful, and adventurous. The color takes on qualities of red and yellow—warm and soothing. The golden glow of sunny yellow evokes happiness and light, while red elicits excitement and passion. Orange is flattering to the skin and is therefore great in bathrooms.

This room lacks natural light but blazing color compensates for the loss. Recessed ceiling lights and light fixtures flanking a mirror provide necessary illumination. You may want to place candles next to the tub for nighttime ambience. Add a moisture loving plant, some pretty colorful bottles filled with fragrant bath products, and a collection of shells from your favorite island. Keep a small magazine rack filled with reading materials to enjoy while bathing. Hang prints or photos from your favorite tropical island.

No man is a hypocrite in his own pleasures.

—JAMES BOSWELL

Simple, relaxed

cottage retreat

Picture a bathroom in a summer cottage. The window is open. Fresh air and sunlight are streaming in. Window treatments are simple and sparse. Painted beadboard surrounds the tub and walls. An old wooden or painted shelf is loaded with shells, pretty towels, bathing paraphernalia, and candles. An Old World–style bench provides storage, seating, and a step stool. Flowers and greenery love it here. Nautical maps or English botanical prints are delicate and fitting. The room exemplifies your simple, relaxed, easygoing attitude toward decorating. With its restful blue-and-white color scheme and utilitarian accessories, functionalism doesn't preempt beauty; it is lovely too.

Come out of the tub exhilarated and ready for a brisk bike ride or a stroll in the coolness of the morning air alongside your flourishing cottage garden.

WALLS
Glidden Paris Night #10BB 42/159

TRIM
Glidden White High Hidding

ACCENTS
White, Pink

ACCESSORY IDEAS
- Beadboard walls/tub surround
- Simple window treatments
- Plants/flowers
- Old wooden shelf, chair, or table

In the cathedral hush of a Quebec Indian summer with the lake drawing into its mirror the fire of the maples, it came to me that to be able to love the mystery surrounding us is the final and only sanction of human existence.

—HUGH MALENNAN

Spirited, fun

WALLS
Benjamin Moore Rosy Blush #2086-30

ACCENTS
White, Maroon, Yellow

ACCESSORY IDEAS
◦ Colorful soaps
◦ Plush striped towels
◦ White cotton rugs
◦ Silver cosmetic containers

tickled pink

This bathroom is small and compact, but mighty in its impact. Subway tiles line the shower and surround the tub. This simple treatment is accented with a splash of color using energizing 1 by 1 inch (3 x 3 cm) orange and red tiles—all interspersed, like thrown confetti. Then, to further emphasize the mini-pink tiles, a delightful coordinating cherry paint color was chosen to cover the walls. While pink has an exciting, attention-getting quality, it has also been shown to calm nerves, and can even lower blood pressure.

Pink works well in the bathroom, especially those without windows or much light. The color creates a flattering, healthy glow to anyone entering the room. The character of this bath is bright, squeaky clean, youthful, spirited, and fun. However, pink makes it feel distinctly feminine, so think of it as "the girl's" bathroom—somewhat romantic and sensual.

The ritual of bathing provides a wonderful opportunity to engage your sense of touch, sight, sound, and scent. Use rejuvenating bath products to add some luxury to your life and turn necessity into pleasure with this dynamic and vivacious pink bathroom.

To be happy at home is the ultimate result of all ambition, the end to which every enterprise and labour tends...

—SAMUEL JOHNSON

Bathroom Furnishing Tips

FURNITURE OPTIONS

- chest as vanity sink

- shelves

- table

- chair

- stool

FOR REFERENCE:

- An unobstructed walkway of 21 inches (63 cm) is needed in front of the toilet, sink, shower, or tub.

- The toilet needs 15 inches (38 cm) of clearance.

- The sink needs 12 inches (30 cm) of clearance.

FOR SINKS AND TUBS:

- Consider a wall-mounted or pedestal sink.

- Turn a vintage flea-market chest or an old sideboard into a sink vanity.

- Check the salvage yard for old porcelain sinks, tubs, and toilets.

- Consider an old or reproduction claw-foot or otherwise free-standing tub.

FOR STORAGE:

- Consider high-tech storage systems if you want a spa-style bath.

- Employ an old scrub pine chest an as accent piece and storage.

- Use a bench or stool to hold small toiletry articles.

- Find an old painted wooden chair to throw towels on.

- If you have space, add a cozy slipcovered chair.

Bathroom Accessorizing Tips

- magazine rack

- old wooden medicine chest

- makeup lights

- table or floor lamps

- moisture-loving plants

- glass or wooden shelves

- refined accents, like a chandelier to add formality

- scatter rugs with nonslip pads

- Shaker-style wooden hooks for towels

- scented candles

- natural sea sponges in a bowl

- lacy or gauzy shower curtains

- beautiful bottles

- large stone bowls for scented soaps

- wire baskets for loofahs, pumice stone

- wooden boxes for oils, herbal soaps

- votive candles

- fishbowls for shells, sea glass

- apothecary jars for cotton balls and swabs

- bathing pillow

- rubber bath toys

- waterproof radio

- sterling silver–topped bottles

- wicker basket for rolls of towels or toilet paper

- perfume bottles

- potpourri

- plant stand for plants or storage

- baker's rack for plants or storage

- bedsheet used for a shower curtain

room structure

The ceiling, walls, and flooring are the backdrop to your room. Let's take a closer look at each element.

CEILING

Some people would like their ceilings to be higher—others (believe it or not) lower. Rooms with high ceilings often have a sense of the grandeur of older homes whether they are old or not. In modern rooms, high ceilings provide an open, spacious feel, whereas lower ceilings promote coziness. Whatever your preference, you can alter the appearance of the height by employing some of the following tricks.

TO CREATE THE LOOK OF A HIGHER CEILING:

- Paint it using a receding color. Cool colors, like pale blue or green, seem to appear farther away and to expand the space between the floor and ceiling.

- Paint a sky and clouds on the entire ceiling, or paint the ceiling white with a sky-blue circle centered overhead. Then add white clouds within the blue circle.

- Incorporate floor-to-ceiling window treatments to emphasize the vertical space.

- Place one or more pieces of tall furniture in the room.

- Paint 4-inch (10 cm)-wide vertical stripes on the walls, or hang wallpaper with a 4-inch (10 cm) stripe using two tones of the same color.

IF YOUR CEILING FEELS TOO HIGH:

- Hang your art at eye level when you are sitting down.

- Paint it in an advancing color. Warm colors, like yellow and orange, appear closer and reduce the visual space between the floor and ceiling.

- Put lighting at low levels.

- Throw colorful rugs on the floor to bring the eye downward.

If your ceiling is plain—no exposed wood beams, moldings, or texture—and you wish it had character, use architectural elements:

- Add an ornamental element to hold your light fixture or just to decorate your ceiling (rosettes and medallions).

- Install moldings where the ceiling meets the walls.

- Cover the entire ceiling with embossed tin and paint it.

WALLS

Walls make up the largest surface area of a room, so they can dramatically affect the mood and atmosphere even without furniture and accessories. Are you satisfied with your existing wall coverings? Do you want to change them? If so, do you prefer wallpaper or paint? Do you want to add character via embellishments on your walls? Look at your walls and use these tips to guide you.

WALLPAPER

- Surprisingly, many large wallpaper designs work well in small rooms because they give an otherwise nondescript space great character.

- Wallpaper conceals imperfect walls, while paint may accentuate imperfections.

- Wallpaper can cover an entire wall or just part of it: from floor to chair-rail height (36 inches above the floor) or from chair rail to ceiling.

- Wallpaper borders located close to the ceiling are generally used in less formal areas, like bedrooms, bathrooms, and children's rooms.

- Wallpaper is historically the preferred wall covering in formal decorating.

- Create unity in a large living room with wallpaper and fabric window treatments in the same large print.

- For beauty and character in a formal or casual setting, consider embossed wallpapers such as anaglypta, which was popular in the early 1900s. The paper is applied and then painted with a gloss-sheened paint. The paper is usually applied to the lower portion of the wall only, up to between 36 and 42 inches (91 and 107 cm) from the floor. A chair rail or wallpaper border separates it from the upper wall, which is painted. Find it at fine wallpaper stores.

- Run a band of an elegant wallpaper border at chair-rail height (36 inches (91 cm) above the floor).

- Test your wallpaper before you make a large investment. Buy one roll and tape it to the wall. Then decide.

- The most economical way to use the most expensive wallpaper, such as hand-printed paper, is to cover only the back panel of a bookshelf or only one portion of a wall, either above or below the chair rail.

PAINTED WALLS

To use a paint palette provided with a recipe in this book, choose the main paint color for the walls, and one or two of the accent colors. The colors are for furnishings and accessories and/or for walls in adjoining rooms. These colors are the basis of your room's color scheme. You can use the main color and the accent color in paler tints or deeper shades. Trim colors are also provided. For detailed information on choosing paint colors, refer to my first book, *The Perfect Palette*, and these tips:

○ Always test paint colors before painting a room. Paint a test patch measuring about 24 by 24 inches (61 by 61 cm). Make sure to use two coats of paint. Do this on at least two of the walls in a room because the light will affect the color on each wall differently. View the test paint colors in daylight and artificial light before deciding. You can buy a small quantity of the paint—usually a quart—for color testing. Some manufacturers sell smaller quantities as testers, and some even rent cans of paint for as little as $1.50 a quart.

○ Wall paint is available in the ever-popular latex (water-based) and alkyd (oil-based) forms. Most people favor latex because it dries quickly (three hours), has no offensive odor, is more environmentally friendly, can be applied easily, and brushes clean up with soap and water.

○ Latex is available in five finishes: high gloss (high sheen, most durable), semigloss (somewhat less shiny, durable), satin (slightly shiny), eggshell (a slight sheen), and flat (no sheen). High gloss may be used on trim, doors, or walls where a shiny surface is desired. People often use flat on walls, but I recommend eggshell or satin, depending on the manufacturer, because they are more washable and durable. Semigloss is almost always used on moldings, unless a very high shine is desired.

○ Alkyd paint is favored by some traditionalists seeking a polished finish. It must be thinned with paint thinner to the consistency of skim milk. You must wait twenty-four hours between applying coats and clean up with paint thinner.

○ When using colors other than the lightest pastels, have your paint dealer tint the primer up to 75 percent. This will give you paint color, rather than just white, on your primer coat, which often significantly reduces the number of color coats you will need to apply, particularly with dark, saturated paint colors.

○ Even if you prefer a pale color palette throughout your home, consider painting one area a rich, saturated color that you love. I often do this in small rooms, entryways, or hallways to create an interesting space. In small rooms, it increases the level of intimacy.

- If you have a chair-rail molding in your room, try using a color from one paint strip for one portion of the wall and a second color (perhaps a tint lighter or a shade darker) from the same paint strip for the other portion of wall.

- Dark rooms look better with colored walls than with white walls, even if you use only a pale tint, because they come alive and assume character.

- Colored ceilings can be a subtle asset. Try a pale yellow or blue.

- When choosing wall paint colors for a room with a multicolored rug, consider choosing the color that is the least apparent in the rug. This creates a good deal of contrast between the walls and the rug. The match is subtle and beautiful.

- When you select the lightest color from a paint strip but find after testing it on the wall that it is still too dark for your taste, have your paint dealer halve the formula. This occurs most often when painting a large wall area, where you see a lot of a color.

- Consider stenciling or hand-painting a favorite quote or poem at the top of the wall around the room like a crown molding. This can be done in any style in any room. For example, a folk art–style dining room can be enhanced with a poem lettered in an appropriate typeface. Calligraphy in gold or silver leaf paint is elegant in a living room.

- Stencil or stamp a repeating pattern, such as starbursts, on the wall.

ARCHITECTURAL EMBELLISHMENTS

- Wainscoting can be casual or formal, depending on the treatment. Tongue-in-groove wood slats from the floor to chair-rail height create a casual, farmhouse quality. Elegant paneling with a raised border yields a more formal look.

- For more visual interest on your walls, add moldings such as baseboards, crown moldings, and chair rails. Chair rails should be 36 inches (91 cm) from the floor.

- Consider wall ornaments made of wood, plaster, or a claylike substance called Compo. These come in a vast array of shapes, designs, and sizes—grapevines, scroll patterns, and so on.

FLOORS

Hardwood is classic, and many people consider it their first choice in flooring. Others favor tile, carpet, and rugs. Look at your floors. Do you like what you see? Do you want to make changes? These tips may help you decide:

- Conceal worn or scarred wood floors with attractive rugs, or paint the floor in solid colors or a patterned design.

- Make a small room feel bigger by leaving the floor as exposed as possible. Use glass-topped tables, slim-legged furniture, and narrow tables. Opt for wall shelves rather than freestanding units.

- Rugs that work well in most homes are vintage or antique Orientals, kilims, chain-stitched rugs, dhurries, hooked, or solid-textured sisal rugs.

- Carpeting in sisal or a wool-sisal blend is ideal for a casual or formal room.

- Dark carpets show every speck of lint.

- Patterned rugs are great dirt concealers.

- Ceramic tile is great in kitchens, baths, and entryways.

- Marble or granite tile is great in entryways and adds to the sleek look of contemporary living and dining rooms.

- Generally, the larger the room, the larger the tile size should be.

- Unify the rooms on one floor of the house by maintaining a single floor covering throughout, such as hardwood. This minimizes contrast and ties the rooms together.

DETAILS

Don't overlook details like doorknobs, handle pulls, and hooks, which can really make a difference in your room's appearance. Refresh the look of your home by replacing ugly old doorknobs, drawer knobs, and door hinges with attractive ones of your own choice. They can blend, highlight, or contrast with your room's decor and are available in many wonderful materials, colors, and shapes, including animals, shells, fruits, and spirals.

creating a color scheme

Creating and adhering to a color scheme is the simplest way to unify the look of the room(s) in your home.

COMBINING COLOR

Principles and theories of color have been used throughout the years to help create color schemes for interior decoration. Here are just a few examples: The monochromatic color scheme calls for shades of only one color within a room, usually with an accent in the complementary color. Polychromatic schemes involve multiple colors within a room. Analogous color schemes combine soft noncontrasting colors (pastels, for example). Triadic schemes combine three colors equidistant from each other on the color wheel.

The simplest and most effective approach to combining color in a room, or even throughout your entire home, is to use two or three colors and perhaps an additional accent color. You can use the paint palettes provided with each recipe in this book as the basis for your color scheme or create your own.

These colors can be used on walls, floors, ceilings, furniture, upholstered pieces, and accessories such as window treatments. Further, you can use them in their darkest versions, lightest versions, or anywhere on the continuum without deviating from the color scheme. Let's say you choose a deep cherry red as the main color and blue as an accent color. You can use a paler, pinker version of the red or a paler version of the blue anywhere in the room without deviating from the color scheme. Visualize it like this:

| pale cherry red (pink) | medium cherry red | deep cherry red |

You can use any of the cherry-red colors, from palest to darkest. This applies to all of your chosen colors for your color scheme. If a fourth or fifth color is introduced as accents, limit them to small areas such as lampshades, vases, and flowers.

Most of the recipes is this book suggest colors based on the recipe's theme. Each recipe suggests a style of fabric, a type of rug, paintings, and many other accessory ideas from which you can isolate colors to become the main colors in your room's color scheme.

For example, an English country theme might suggest floral chintz fabrics. You would choose floral chintz fabrics that you love, then isolate two or three colors from the fabric. These colors become the core of your color scheme. The following example helps you better understand this process.

Okavango, an African-inspired living room recipe (see page 31), evokes images of wildlife, wilderness, and papyrus trees. Choose colors from related traditional fabrics such as batiks and kente cloth—perhaps the golden straw color of woven baskets and a tribal red or sizzling orange. Of the two or three colors you select, none needs to dominate. All your main colors can be used in fairly equal amounts, or one can be a main color and the others can be accents.

Remember, the tints and shades of each color can vary from room to room. Color is a wonderful tool for unifying the decorating flow of a home. Choose your favorites, and you will be constantly delighted.

textiles, windows, lighting, and picture hanging

Before you commit to fabrics for your upholstery, slipcovers, window treatments, rugs, and other accessories, bring home sample swatches. You can avoid expensive mistakes by trying out the swatches in the room. Your fabrics will convey your personal style—casual, formal, or somewhere in between. Your color scheme and the recipe's theme will unify the look in the room. Incorporate pattern and texture as suggested in the recipe. Choose lighter-weight fabrics for a cool spring or summer feel and heavier fabrics for a warmer feel. If you already have a perfectly good sofa or overstuffed chair that is somewhat dated or needs a facelift, consider adding interesting textured or print pillows and a nice throw blanket; this may be all you need to give the furniture a fresh, updated look. Ready-made slipcovers, which are sold in a wide variety of fabrics, are another option. They are readily available in standard sizes through home store catalogs. Here are fabric examples to get you started.

FABRICS

NATURAL FABRICS

Cotton: Strong fiber that blends well with other fibers. Machine washable and inexpensive.

Wool: Strong fiber that insulates. Drapes easily. Must be dry cleaned and is moderately expensive.

Linen: A strong and slightly textured, stiff fiber with a natural luster. Must be dry cleaned to preserve appearance and is expensive.

Silk: Lustrous fiber that drapes elegantly. Most require dry cleaning; some are hand washable. All are expensive.

SYNTHETIC FABRICS

Rayon: Drapes well and blends well with other fibers. Can be made to look like natural fibers. A weak fiber that shrinks and stretches unless treated correctly. Some must be dry cleaned; others can be hand washed. Inexpensive.

Acetate: Appears silklike and drapes well. It is a weak fiber and must be treated correctly. Dry clean unless the label indicates hand washing. Moderately inexpensive.

Acrylic: Has a wool-like texture and is a fairly strong fiber. Not durable, especially when wet. Tends to stretch and pill. Hand wash unless label suggests otherwise. Moderately expensive.

Polyester: A strong fiber that doesn't shrink or stretch. Can be any texture from slick to nubby. Most can be machine washed. Moderately inexpensive.

Nylon: Strong fiber that is lustrous and looks glassy. Most can be machine washed. Moderately inexpensive.

Olefin: Lightweight with good bulk, a strong fiber and a good insulator. Best used as part of a fabric blend or as lining. Machine washable. Moderately inexpensive.

Note: Casual cotton fabrics and synthetics, such as acetates, are durable, moderately inexpensive, and great for upholstery.

COMMON FABRIC TERMS

Brocade: A fabric with a raised pattern that looks almost like embroidery. Usually seen in formal settings.

Chenille: A thick fabric with needle-punched designs that was commonly used for bedspreads in the 1960s. It is now often used on robes and casual upholstery.

Chintz: A plain-weave cotton with a shine or glaze. Crisp, good for drapery and table covers. Works equally well in formal and casual settings.

Damask: Contrasts satin sheen and dull sheen pattern within the fabric. It looks identical on both sides of the fabric, so it is great for window swags.

Lush and formal, great for upholstery. Can be made to look casual when used as oversized slipcovers. Washed damask has a casual, crinkly look.

Matelassé: Embossed fabric traditionally used for formal bedspreads. It works equally well as upholstery in casual or formal decor.

Moiré: Shiny fabric that looks as if it has a wood grain or water stain. It is very formal. Good on drapery, great with antique furniture. Gives texture without a pattern.

Plissé: Looks like seersucker, only larger, with puckered stripes. Casual but workable in a formal setting.

Strie: Varied warp-thread colors create an irregular, streaked look. Good in casual or formal settings.

Taffeta: Crisp plain-weave fabric; excellent for window coverings because it retains its shape. Good in casual or formal settings.

Tapestry: Thick fabric with pictorial designs. Can be used in casual or formal settings.

Toile de Jouy: Fabric with a picture printed onto it in a single color on top of a neutral base color. Works well on large pieces. Can be used in formal or casual setting.

Twill: Tightly woven with a diagonal ridge, like denim and herringbone fabrics. Casual.

Velvet: Shiny, feels like fur, usually in rich, jewel-toned colors. A durable, formal fabric.

PATTERN

Consider these tips on the use of pattern in fabrics.

- In general, it is best to distribute pattern evenly around a room.

- Bright patterns and bold colors magnify the proportions of the furniture they are on.

- Small prints tend to get lost in large rooms. They look better in smaller rooms and on smaller pieces of furniture and accessories, like pillows and lampshades.

- Busy, patterned fabrics work best when window treatments and walls are pattern free.

- A one-pattern scheme (using only one pattern on fabric within a room) is easily manageable even for the novice. The print should be large and bold enough to carry the room. Often, an equally bold wall color is the best way to balance the room, but it is not necessary. If you are planning to paint the walls, choose your paint color from among those in the fabric.

- A simple way to add interest to a one-pattern scheme is to incorporate one or more accessories with their own pattern, such as an Oriental, chain-stitched, or hooked rug or a lovely vintage quilt.

- A two-pattern scheme might include a small check or stripe mixed with a color-related larger floral. Mixing a check or a stripe with a floral is a fail-safe approach to a two-pattern scheme. For example, combine a floral sofa with striped toss pillows.

- For a three-pattern scheme, choose your favorite pattern—perhaps a bold floral—and use it in approximately 60 percent of the room. Choose a second color-related fabric that is different in scale, perhaps a narrow stripe, and use it in approximately 30 percent of the room. Finally, choose a third color-related fabric of a different scale, perhaps a midsize stripe, mini-floral, or small check, and use it in approximately 10 percent of the room. Solid-color fabrics can always be used in multiple-pattern schemes.

- For multiple-pattern schemes, you can buy fabrics from a premixed collection. These are readily available in most fabric stores. Alternatively, select patterns from the same color family.

- In multiple-pattern schemes, vary the size of the patterns from large to medium to small. Try to use each pattern at least three times within the room.

- Checks and plaids make great filler prints alongside florals.

TEXTURE

A novice choosing to avoid bold colors and patterns can achieve a finished look with neutral colors in soft and fine textures, hard and rugged textures, or a mixture of both. For a formal look, choose soft and fine textures. Moving along the continuum toward casual, you can mix the textures. For example, mix smooth fabrics with rough fabrics. Just as you mix textured furniture, like rough wicker chairs with smooth wooden tables, to create a more casual look, you mix accessories. Try placing a textured rug over a smooth floor; throw a textured afghan on a smooth-fabric sofa. These opposites create more interest.

WINDOWS

Choose window treatments based on your personal need for:

- privacy
- noise barrier
- letting light in or blocking it out
- keeping out heat or cold
- grandly decorated decor
- framing a window
- framing a view
- blocking a view
- elongating a window
- elongating the ceiling
- making a window the focal point in the room

I usually leave window treatments for last because I prefer lots of light coming in while I am working on my rooms, and I often find that I don't need window treatments at all. When I do, I see them as a finishing touch. However, if you want grand, formal window treatments, dress your windows during the initial stages of the accessorizing process. Remember, your choice of fabric determines in large part how formal or casual your window treatment will be. These guidelines can help you get started.

MORE FORMAL

- balloon shades
- valances and swags
- draperies with tassels, ropes, rosettes, pleats, fancy trims
- Roman shades
- chiffon or washed-silk sheers

MORE CASUAL

- valances
- tab curtains
- Roman shades
- washed-silk sheers

- wooden venetian blinds (narrow or wide, with colored fabric tapes)
- metal blinds
- plantation shutters (floor to ceiling)
- bamboo blinds
- matchstick blinds (hung inside window frame)
- café curtains (cover only the lower portion of the window)
- For inexpensive curtains, try using new, freshly ironed sheets. Use the top hem as the rod pocket, or sew on standard curtain rings.
- Curtain fabric should be $2\frac{1}{2}$ to 3 times as wide as the window.
- Lightweight fabrics are best for creating a draping effect or pooling on the floor.
- Heavier fabrics create a more angled, structured look.
- Use blackout linings to keep light out.
- For better room insulation from heat and cold, get Thermaline linings.
- Extend window treatments beyond the bounds of small windows to make them look taller or wider.
- Try layering fabric for more interesting window treatments. For an elegant look, layer a sheer, translucent organza over a silk jacquard.
- Try cotton netting in grid patterns for fuller but still understated curtains. Layer a heftier grid pattern over a lacy pattern for double fullness.
- Choose interesting decorative finials to enhance your windows. They can tie into the theme of the room— seashells in a nautical-themed room, for example.
- If you have three or more side-by-side windows on one wall, avoid finials to prevent a cluttered look.

- Create a café curtain with a narrow rod and clip-on rings that open when you pinch them and clamp shut onto the fabric when you let go. Fabric should be $2\frac{1}{2}$ times the width of the window for an airy look.
- A simple but attractive treatment: Hang fabrics flat without any pleats or folds.
- For a curtain to spill or puddle onto the floor, add 6 to 8 inches (15 to 20 cm) to the length of fabric.
- Keep dormer window treatments simple. Avoid strong colors and patterns. Consider long sheers, wooden shutters, or fabric blinds.
- Wooden rods that look best have a diameter of $2\frac{1}{2}$ to 3 inches (6 to 8 cm).
- For ease of installation, buy a tension rod. Springs hold it in place in the window frame without installing hardware.
- Buy stained-glass paint and paint the window in interesting patterns. To dress up a simple window treatment, use pretty trim or embellishments, like beads or buttons.
- Plain wood venetian blinds give a modern, clean, simple look.
- Have your fabric laminated and create a roller shade.
- Consider swing-out rods, with fabric panels attached to the rods at the top and bottom. They swing open and closed like shutters.

LIGHTING

Like every other element in your decorating, the quality of light in your rooms dramatically affects the atmosphere. It deserves a second look when you are redecorating because dingy, yellow cast light can compromise the desired effect. Lighting should be chosen based on your personal needs and preferences. Let's address basic lighting issues, keeping this goal in mind: You want your lighting to look as natural as possible.

- The two most common types of light in homes are fluorescent, which is flat, cool, and often used in kitchens, and incandescent, which includes standard lightbulbs and the harsher, bright light of halogen lamps.
- The quality of light is determined by the type of light it is, its brightness and intensity (which is determined by the wattage of the bulb), and where you place it in the room.
- Most rooms require some form of ambient light that covers the entire room.
- The light fixture hangs on or near the ceiling.
- Track lighting (in white or black) with spotlights is compatible with all design styles.
- Recessed lighting is also compatible with all design styles and is completely unobtrusive. It also makes ceilings look higher.

Task lighting is just what it sounds like: lighting for specific tasks, like reading, food preparation, or dining. Choose fixtures you love. Examples of task lighting are:

- desk lamps
- chandeliers (for both ambient and task lighting)
- bedside lamps
- undercabinet or undershelf lights

Accent lights are purely decorative, although they do provide additional light as well. Patterned and glass lampshades give a warmer look than solid cream-colored shades do.

- sconces (wall-hung lights, usually in pairs)

- spotlights
- torchères (standing floor lamps that shine upward)
- lamps
- chandeliers

PICTURE HANGING

Before you bang any nails into the wall, arrange the items on the floor, make paper patterns, and tape them to the walls. Then move them around until you are satisfied.

The most common mistake people make is hanging art too high. Try to hang it at eye level or lower. Use these tips for guidance on picture hanging:

- Keep wall plaster intact while hammering holes by placing Scotch tape over the wall where the nail will go.
- Hang like items with like items: oils with oils, watercolors with watercolors, and so on.
- Consider framing two pictures similarly or identically and hanging them side by side as a pair. Pairs of items add to a balanced look.
- Two different-sized but related pictures look good hung as a pair, the smaller one above the other.
- Hang three similar pictures in a vertical or horizontal row.
- Hang four related pictures two over two.
- Hang small groupings of pictures stacked two or three high.
- Align groupings of three or more pictures along the bottom of their frames.
- Art on different walls can be hung at different heights.
- Generally, walls wider than they are high call for horizontal groupings.
- Narrow wall spaces welcome vertical arrangements of frames.

- Keep the space between frames equal, allowing at least 1 to 2 inches (3 to 5 cm); otherwise, paintings seem to drift on the wall.
- To create intimacy, hang pictures low to visually link them with furniture.
- The frame and mat (the border between the art and the frame) should complement rather than compete with the pictures.
- Traditional art is usually framed with carved wood and multilayered mats.
- The framed image, not a room's color palette, should guide you in selecting the mat color.
- Mats in dark hues are dramatic.
- Light mats emphasize the art.
- Mats should be at least twice as wide as frames.
- Tiny pictures with oversize mats have an appealing, museum-style look.
- Use oversized mats when hanging pictures on wallpaper—at least 3 to 4 inches (8 to 10 cm) wide—to keep framed images separated.
- One big framed poster or painting can provide a focal point for an entire room.
- Wrap a series of similar prints around a corner to create intimacy.
- Hang a favorite picture beside a doorway so you can enjoy it often.
- When hanging mirrors, make sure you like what is being reflected.

Not many sounds in life...exceed in interest a knock at the door.

—CHARLES LAMB

entryways and hallways

ENTRYWAYS

In some homes, the entryway is large enough to be treated as a room in its own right. In other homes, the entryway may be tiny or disjointed.

The entry area functions as a place to take off and hang your coat and, perhaps, toss your keys, mail, and sunglasses. It is also a place to welcome guests, and it provides their first impression of your home. This area probably receives a lot of wear and tear, so choose furnishings that are durable and easy to keep clean.

Regardless of your entry's size or shape, it should reflect the same style as the rest of the house, even if you are merely passing through. You may choose to carry a recipe from an adjoining room into the entryway. In this case, decorate and accessorize according to the recipe.

Remember, a piece or two of large-scale furniture often works well even in small spaces. Make your entry feel as though it is part of the house. If your entry is large, identify or create one or more focal points, then place furniture and accessories near and around it.

Think of a typical hotel lobby, warm and inviting. Bring some of those elements into the area, even if it is small. These may include any grouping of the following items:

- upholstered chairs, perhaps in tapestry fabric, flanking a lovely side table

- side table (should be shallower and several inches taller than a conventional dining table in foyer area)

- plants (palms are perfect, or a tabletop plant)

- potted flowering plants in season

- inventive lighting, especially a chandelier, spotlights, or sconces

- patterned area rug, such as an Oriental or hooked style

- drapes on windows flanking entry door

- topiaries or potted plants flanking entry door

- mirrors

- groupings of wall art going up stairway walls and throughout entry

- painted floor design

- interesting wallpaper

- wall shelf to display a collection

- if no closet, a bench, coat rack, shelf, or row of wooden pegs for mittens, hats, coats

- baskets and boxes for additional paraphernalia

- umbrella stand

- chest or console flanked by two chairs

- desk and chair

If a small entryway contains stairs, enhance the area by painting the vertical part of each step (the risers) in a lovely, unusual color, like midnight blue or red. Use alkyd (oil-based) paint thinned with paint thinner for better durability. Apply two to three coats, waiting twenty-four hours between each.

HALLWAYS

- Long hallways that seem tunnel-like can be made more attractive with 5-foot (1.5 m) built-in bookshelves extending the length of one wall, or the width between two doors.

- Divide a long hallway in two with a floor-length curtain panel suspended by wooden rings from a pretty rod. Pull the fabric to one side and hold in place with a tieback.

- Hang a large collection of beautifully framed mirrors.

- Demi-lune (half-moon) tables are great in long hallways.

- Long, narrow console tables work well in hallways.

- Overscaled objects and a lamp clustered on a hall table form an instant focal point. Try tall vases, a stack of decorative boxes or books, or a few small objects. Hang an artwork grouping above the table.

- Rug runners should be no more than 4 inches (10 cm) narrower than the hallway on each side.

PAINT COLOR INDEX

PAGE 6
Glidden Summery Savory #70GY 41/424

PAGE 9, right
Walls: Benjamin Moore #2015-70 Apricot Ice

Trim: Benjamin Moore #HC-119 Kittery Point Green

Door: Benjamin Moore #2014-40 Peachy Keen

PAGE 9, left
Chairs: Laura Ashley Fuchsia #1331 636

PAGE 11
Benjamin Moore #2029-40 Stem Green

PAGE 13
Laura Ashley #1331 487 Summer Pudding

Laura Ashley #5392 568 Oatmeal

Laura Ashley #5392 485 White

PAGE 14
Benjamin Moore #AC-27 Galveston Gray

PAGE 17, right
Laura Ashley Fuchsia #1324 144

Laura Ashley Pale Delphinium #1635 523

Laura Ashley Chambray #5393 111

Laura Ashley Lavender #1213 420

Laura Ashley Forget-me-knot #1213 438

Laura Ashley Peony #1331 495

PAGE 24
Benjamin Moore #2073-30 Passion Plum

PAGE 44
Benjamin Moore #2019-50 Lemon Drops

PAGE 47
Benjamin Moore Brilliant White

PAGE 49
Glidden Spring Awakening #50YY 34/250

PAGE 50
Benjamin Moore #2137-30 Durango

PAGE 64
Benjamin Moore #2116-30 Cabernet

PAGE 67
Glidden Autumn Haze #45YY 67/120

PAGES 68 & 82
Glidden Skyline #70BB 65/006

PAGES 80 & 83, bottom right
Bookcase: Glidden Turkish Brown #20YY 09/175

PAGE 84
Laura Ashley Pale Delphinium #1635 523

PAGE 100
Walls: Glidden Country Lane #71GY 67/245

Bed: Glidden Summer Savory #70GY 41/424

PAGE 102
Glidden Surfside #10GG 74/087

PAGE 104
Sherwin Williams #SW1537 Boysenberry

PAGE 112
Benjamin Moore #2079-40 Springtime Bloom

Benjamin Moore #2078-70 Pink Peony

PAGE 116
Glidden Lavender Twilight #38BB 69/096

PAGE 126
Benjamin Moore #2150-30 Savannah Green

PAGE 128
Benjamin Moore #2067-40 Blue Lapis

PAGE 129
Benjamin Moore #2000-10 Red

PAGE 130
Glidden Sun Rays #29YY 66/537

PAGE 131
Floor: Benjamin Moore Heritage Red

PAGE 132
Benjamin Moore #2064-30 ol' Blue Eyes

PAGE 138
Pratt and Lambert #1021 Cranberry

PAGE 139
Benjamin Moore #2156-50 Asbury Sand

Benjamin Moore #2034-40 Cedar Green

Some of the furniture and accessories used in these rooms were graciously provided by:

Concord Museum Gift Shop
200 Lexington Road
Concord, MA 01742
978-369-5477

The Cottage on Monument Square
15 Monument Street
Concord, MA 01742
978-369-2000

The Concord Flower Shop
109 Thoreau Street
Concord, MA 01742
978-369-2404

Open Market
28 Walden Street
Concord, MA 01742
978-369-8664

Powers Gallery
342 Great Road
Acton, MA 01742
978-263-5105

Services for photo styling for some of the rooms were provided by:

Jean Carter and Seri Ling
Studio 742
Concord, MA 01742
978-369-0763

Photo styling for the following recipes:
Okavango, Swan Lake, Music Under the Stars, Island, Coastal Dreams, Baby Mine, and Matisse's Colors.

Hairstyling for author photo:

Maddy Gersh, Hairstylist
Eccoli Hair Design
1707 Massachusetts Avenue
Lexington, MA 02173
781-863-1994

PAINT COMPANIES

Benjamin Moore
51 Chestnut Ridge Road
Montvale, NJ 07645
800-344-0400
www.benjaminmoore.com

California Paints
169 Waverly Street
Cambridge, MA 02139-0007
800-225-1141
www.californiapaints.com

Glidden
ICI Paints
Cleveland, Ohio 44115
1-800-GLIDDEN
www.glidden.com

Pittsburgh Paints
PPG Industries, Inc.
One PPG Place
Pittsburgh, PA 15272
800-441-9695
www.ppgaf.com

Pratt and Lambert
(The Sherwin-Williams Co.)
1-800-BUYPRAT
www.prattandlambert.com

Sherwin-Williams Company
101 Prospect Avenue
Cleveland, OH 44115
216-566-2000
www.sherwin-williams.com

Laura Ashley Ltd
27 Bagleys Lane
Fulham, SW6 2QA
UK
0870-562-2116
www.lauraashley.com

PAINTED FURNITURE

Maine Cottage Furniture
P.O. Box 935
Yarmouth, ME 04096
207-846-1430
www.mainecottage.com

FABRIC

Zimmer & Rohde
Etamine
www.zimmer-rohde.com

Courtesy of Laura Ashley Ltd., 3; 17 (right)

Guillaume DeLaubier, 8, 132; 139

Tria Giovan, 24; 114

Courtesy of Glidden, an ICI Paints brand, 7; 9 (left); 34; 48; 49; 66 (top & middle); 67; 68; 71; 76; 79; 80; 82; 83; 100; 103; 107; 113; 116; 117

Sam Gray, 30; 55; 66 (bottom); 96; 99; 108; 115; 124; 125; 128; 129

Tim Imrie/Abode, 59

RayMain/www.mainstreamimages .co.uk, 6; 44; 112; 119; 123

Courtesy of Maine Cottage Furniture, 9 (right); 11; 23; 38; 41

Courtesy of Benjamin Moore & Co., 141

Eric Roth, 26; 29; 37; 42; 56; 60; 63; 64; 75; 87; 88; 91; 92; 95; 111; 131 (left); 138

Eric Roth/Astrid Vigeland Design, 47

Brian Vanden Brink, 14; 50; 84

Brian Vanden Brink/Stephen Blatt Architects, 126

Brian Vanden Brink/Quinn Evans, Architect, 102

Brian Vanden Brink/Stephen Foote, Architect, 13; 52

Brian Vanden Brink/Weston & Hewitson Architects, 104

Brian Vanden Brink/Mark Hutker & Associates Architects, 131 (right)

Brian Vanden Brink/Dominic Mercadante, Architect, 33; 120

Brian Vanden Brink/Jack Silverio Architect, 130

Simon Whitmore/Abode, 72

Courtesy of Zimmer + Rohde, 17 (left)

About the Author

Bonnie Krims is the author of *The Perfect Palette* (Warner Books) and *The Perfectly Painted House* (Rockport Publishers). She is a nationally recognized professional paint color consultant.

Please visit Bonnie Krims's Web site: www.theperfectpalette.com

email: Bkrims@aol.com

Fax: 978-371-6432

Acknowledgments

Special thanks to Penny Rosser and Kate Krims. Your collective knowledge, talent, insight, and support allowed this book to take shape. Thanks to Betsy Gammons for all the help with photography and to Winnie Prentiss, my publisher, for holding it all together, through thick and thin. My heartfelt gratitude to Diane Tuttle (Nui). Thanks to my husband, Peter, for his confidence and support. Finally, thanks to my children, Elise and Maxwell, for making me so very proud.